T

Granny's Household Hints

GRANNY'S HOUSEHOLD HINTS

*Traditional Tips
for a Clean, Green Home*

BRENDA EVANS

SPHERE

First published in Great Britain by Sphere in 2010
Copyright © Omnipress Limited 2010

The moral right of the author has been asserted.

A CIP catalogue record for this book
is available from the British Library.

ISBN 978-1-84744-410-3

Typeset in Great Britain by Omnipress Limited
Printed and bound in India

Sphere
An imprint of
Little, Brown Book Group
100 Victoria Embankment
London EC4Y 0DY

An Hachette UK Company
www.hachette.co.uk

www.littlebrown.co.uk

DISCLAIMER

The information in this book is intended as a guide only and
should not be relied upon as the sole source of information relating
to its content. It is sold with the understanding that the author and publisher
are not liable for the misconception or misuse of information provided.
The information provided is in no way intended as a substitute for medical
counselling and any DIY instructions should be carefully reviewed before
undertaking any project.

Contents

Home Sweet Home

Granny sweeps the kitchen floor
Using a broom made from straw
And sprinkles damp tea leaves around
To pick up the dust on the ground.

Memories are triggered by certain smells, sounds or situations and for me the smell of bread baking will always take me back to my summer holidays spent in North Devon with my grandparents. They lived in the small village of Shobrooke in a tiny thatched cottage without any of the modern luxuries we take for granted today. In fact they didn't even have running water in the house. Granny used to take my hand early in the morning and take me to the back garden where she pumped water by hand into an old tin bucket for our morning wash and breakfast needs. The toilet, or 'linny' as grandad called it, was also in the back garden, so you always made sure you went before going to bed because there was no way as kids we would have been brave enough to venture out in the dark. Like many children, I was scared of creepy-crawlies, so every time I had to use the linny I made sure I kept my eyes closed, just in case there was a 'tarantula' lurking in the corner. My sister always said I was prone to exaggeration!

You might think the poem on the opposite page a little strange, but this is exactly what my 'Tiny Gran' used to do to help keep the dust down. She said it wasn't healthy to breathe in a lot of dust and to stop it settling on all the shelves and furniture while she swept, she used damp tea leaves to help catch the dust before it flew into the air. I have also heard of people using damp sawdust which had exactly the same effect.

The only form of heating in the cottage was a wood stove in the front room and the old cast-iron oven which was actually built into the thick stone walls. It had two ovens with heavy doors and a hot plate on the top which was covered by two lids, much the same as the modern-day Agas. The handles on the lids were usually too hot to touch, so an old metal lever was left on a chair at the side of the stove just for this purpose. On top of the stove granny kept two old flat irons as the cottage did not have electricity, so washday was arduous. I remember granny clutching her back after a particularly long session with the washboard. Even on very hot days, granny would have to stand beside the oven to iron, as it was a constant cycle of heating, pressing, and reheating, all the time keeping the irons spotlessly clean so there was nothing to soil her beautiful white linens. To keep the baseplate of the irons free from any build-up of starch, granny always kept a cloth soaked in white vinegar and regularly wiped them after each round of ironing.

The oven kept the downstairs warm and there was always a pot of porridge bubbling on the top whenever we came down for breakfast and an old kettle that was constantly on the boil. Above the oven was a wooden clothes-drying rack which was hoisted up and down on pulleys using a waxed rope. This rack was used on days when it was too wet or cold to use the washing line in the garden, which was tied between two trees and held up by an old wooden clothes prop.

There was an old blackboard on the side of the scullery wall which had a list of PINK jobs and BLUE jobs, which meant nothing to me for my first few years. When eventually I was old enough to query the list, granny told me that 'pink' were jobs that she had to do and 'blue' were ones for grandad. I used to like watching grandad chop the wood for the fire and the oven, but he used to make me sit at a distance so that no bits of sawdust flew into my eyes. Another of his jobs was emptying the ashes out of the grate and then taking them out to the garden and scattering them under his rose bushes and on the vegetable patch to help enrich the soil. I can still see the old rug in front of the fire, full of little burn holes from hot embers that used to drop as grandad emptied the grate. He always got a ticking off from granny for not being careful enough.

Another of his jobs was to go to the farm down the bottom of the lane and collect the milk. He had a small metal milk churn with a handle, which was washed out each morning and then taken to collect the next day's supply. On the weeks that granny made butter, grandad would have to make more than one trip and I remember him grumbling under his breath about having to climb back up the hill with a heavy churn. I always loved the days that granny churned the butter; as with most things, it was done by hand.

With no fridge to keep food fresh, our ancestors had to devise ways of stopping food from going off. The larder shelves were packed with jars of pickles and preserves, and there were also large meat hooks on the wall where meat was hung up after being preserved in salt. Grandad had also made his own smokery in the back garden, well away from the house because granny moaned about the smoke coming in through the back door. I remember the smell to this day and the fact that there was always smoked sausage, bacon, and ham for lunch – things that we just took for granted as kids.

Eggs were fresh straight from grandad's allotment. I used to take great delight in searching for eggs that had been laid in the strangest places by those hens who didn't like to lay in the straw-lined coop. One of their favourite places was underneath an old wheelbarrow that grandad kept propped up in the corner by the shed. Or between the blades of an antique rotovator that grandad kept for turning the soil at the start of the growing season. Eggs were kept in an earthenware crock in the scullery, and they were eaten so quickly they never had time to go off. My sister and I would always squeal with delight if we were the one lucky enough to get the double yolker for breakfast or tea.

Sunday lunch was always roast chicken and it was delicious. It never actually occurred to me where the chicken came from and I can remember being horrified when I caught granny holding a chicken upside down by its legs with her other arm raised, ready to decapitate it. I screamed and ran back into the house and vowed I would never eat chicken again. This didn't last very long – I think a week at the most – because as soon as I got the smell of it roasting, my taste buds got the better of me.

There were no local shops, just a post office that sold newspapers and a few penny sweets. Shopping trips were rare, but when granny ran out of flour or sugar we used to don our Sunday best and get on the bus to Crediton. Grandad didn't own a car, just an old motorbike with a rickety old sidecar which we used to love to ride in as kids. There was a hole in the canvas roof which granny had stuffed an old terry towelling nappy in to stop the rain from making the seats wet. Granny used to love riding pillion in her youth, but as the years advanced and her joints ached from too much hard work (or so she said) she told us she would rather have the luxury of the bus. Crediton wasn't big by any means, but it did have a J. Sainsbury's store – nothing like those we know today though. It was just one long room with a counter running down either side. You didn't help yourself; this was much more of a social occasion, making small talk with the man behind the counter. Everything came wrapped in brown paper or paper bags – not a piece of plastic in sight. Money was in short supply and granny's shopping list was not very long.

There was no browsing the shelves and filling your baskets with luxury items that took your fancy.

Vegetables were grown at home and she had the knack of making food go a long way. Nothing was ever wasted – if the sausages weren't finished at breakfast they would be dished up in toad-in-the-hole for dinner. Any meat left over was used in a shepherd's pie or home-made rissoles and you never sat down to afternoon tea without a cake taking pride of place at the centre of the table. Fish was a real treat and was obtained from the fish van that used to come once a fortnight on a Friday. Granny would send me down the lane to wait outside the post office with my 1s 3d to buy some fresh mackerel.

Times might have been hard for my grandparents, but they were happy. Granny had a cure for everything and because as kids we spent so much time outdoors I don't ever remember taking to my bed while I was staying in Devon. Cholesterol levels and blocked arteries were never considered as we tucked into our syrup pudding or scones piled high with strawberry jam and granny's clotted cream. Maybe it was because we played hard, slept well, and were well away from the stresses and bustle of city life that we kept healthy, who knows, but granny certainly seemed to have the answer. The modern generation could take a leaf out of granny's book and learn to take life a little more slowly and enjoy what we do have instead of always wanting more. I remember some of my first Christmases and sitting waiting patiently in front of the tree to open my presents. Two or three at the most, but they were so special, and many of which I have kept for my own children and grandchildren. One in particular was a little wooden tractor that my grandad had made in his old shed and grandma had lovingly made little bales of hay to go in the trailer on the back. The bales didn't survive, but the tractor is still going strong to this day.

Chapter One

Granny's
Cleaning Clues

Clean as a Whisker

Granny's day it never ends
A pie to cook, a sock to mend
Wash the clothes, sweep the floor
Push the geese out of the door
Granny's life was a bit of a trial
And yet she always had time to smile.

I don't remember granny ever taking a rest, well not during the day. She was on the go from dawn to dusk, but she always had time to listen and time to teach. She used to pull an old wooden chair up to the kitchen table, tell me to stand on it and then put her apron round my middle and tie it round several times. She showed me how to bake many things, but I especially enjoyed being allowed to put the raisin buttons down the middle of the gingerbread men. She showed me how to get a shine on glass and a sheen on wood and never once did she put on a pair of rubber gloves to protect her skin.

Granny did not use proprietary cleaners laden with bleach and other products that claimed to work miracles. Her cleaners were everyday products like vinegar, bicarbonate of soda, and lemons, and a lot of elbow grease. Today, with the worry of global warming and polluting the earth on which we live, people are becoming more conscientious about tipping toxic chemicals down their sinks. With the help of this book you will be able to learn how to clean your whole house and leave it sparkling and sanitized at the same time, without the use of any harsh products. In this chapter I am going to give you loads of useful hints on how to get the best effect for the least effort. Don't be put off; it worked for granny and it will most definitely work for you.

It won't cost you a fortune and you can be sure you will already have the ingredients you need for a cleaner, greener home.

You will find the mention of a product called borax crops up time and time again and it is something your mother or grandmother would probably have kept permanently in the laundry room. It is made from a natural mineral, sodium borate, which was discovered over four thousand years ago. It is non-toxic, safe to use, and was originally used to soften water and make white clothes brighter. It has many uses, as it has both disinfecting and deodorizing properties and is also great for preserving cut flowers.

Hints on Keeping Your Home Green and Clean

- During the summer your house is constantly being aired by either a window or a back door being left open for most of the day. In the winter, however, we tend to shut our houses up and with the added insulation of double glazing, very little fresh air enters our rooms. Fresh air is essential for keeping upholstery, carpets, beds, and curtains smelling fresh, so even on those very cold days allow a quick blast of air into the room while you are doing the cleaning. If you are like me, you will probably be too hot anyway and be glad of the cool air.

- Try to cut down on the amount of dust in your house by removing any clutter like old newspapers and magazines, or a pile of toys that haven't been played with for a long time. I work by the rule that if I haven't used anything within the last year then it is time to get rid of it. Anything that is worth recycling, like old clothes, toys, shoes, appliances, etc, should either be taken to a charity shop or given to a recycling centre. Don't just dump them in the dustbin as they will only add to the growing problems at our landfill sites. Your unwanted goods may be just what someone else is looking for. If you don't mind getting up early you could always take a load to a boot sale and earn yourself a few pounds at the same time. Unwanted furniture can also be donated to organizations like the Salvation Army who pass it on to families who are in need of some decent pieces.

- Make sure everyone takes their shoes off before tramping through the house, as this will cut down a lot on your dust and dirt.

- Most households today use sponges for cleaning or washing up that are made out of polyester or plastic. These are not biodegradable and add to the problem at our landfill sites. Instead, try to buy cellulose sponges which are available at natural food stores. These are biodegradable, environmentally friendly and are made using wood pulp and cotton from sustained resources. They actually soak up spills a lot faster as they are more absorbent and are perfect for removing make-up and for use with cosmetics, too.

- We spend a lot of our time in the bedroom so it is important to keep it as dust-free and clean as possible. Start by turning your mattress every couple of months (a job for two people) and then giving it a good vacuum in between. Vacuum the carpet regularly, keep surfaces clean and try to keep your pets out of this room as they can quickly add to a build-up of dirt and hairs.

- Use only environmentally friendly products for cleaning, as many of the proprietary toilet cleaners, drain cleaners, and oven cleaners in particular are extremely toxic. Avoid any products that contain ammonia, chlorine, or petroleum-based chemicals, as these can lead to respiratory irritation, skin rashes, headaches, and other complaints.

- When you clean your house leave the vacuuming until last, as this will give the dust time to settle before the final clean.

A–Z of Cleaning

● **ABRASIVE CLEANER**

Bicarbonate of soda and salt are both mild abrasives that can easily take the place of commercial scrubbing powders. Salt is slightly more abrasive but it is still gentle enough for most surfaces.

● **AIR FRESHENER**

In a spray bottle mix some water and a few drops of your favourite essential oil and use when you need to get rid of a nasty niff. You can change the scent whenever you fancy and it is safe to use on everything.

Leave a few small bowls containing some bicarbonate of soda mixed with some vinegar or lemon juice around the house; these will quickly absorb any nasty odours.

● **ALL-PURPOSE CLEANER**

Instead of buying proprietary brands of cleaners for the bathroom and kitchen, why not make one all-purpose one which you can use on anything. Mix about three tablespoons of washing soda in 1 litre of warm water. Wash off with clean water.

Alternatively, for a no-rinse cleaner, mix equal parts of white vinegar and water and keep it in a handy plastic spray bottle.

● **BABY WIPES**

If you have a young baby in the house then you are certain to have a few packets of these lying around, but did you know they are great at cleaning stainless steel appliances in the kitchen? Or, if you prefer, wipe the appliance over with a piece of kitchen towel and a few drops of baby oil. Both ways will produce a lovely shine.

Baby wipes are also good for cleaning leather furniture and radiators, especially those hard-to-reach vents on the top, spills on the floor and worktops. Make sure you buy the ones that do not have any alcohol in them, though.

BATHTUB RINGS
To get rid of the ring of scum around the bathtub, rub it with some neat lemon juice and then wipe off with a sponge.

BLOODSTAINS
If you have got bloodstains on clothing from, say, a cut finger or a nosebleed, remove the garment and soak in some salty water straight away. Wring out and wash as normal.

BUFF UP THOSE BOOTS
Winter can take a toll on your boots and shoes, especially if you are like me and love to walk, even when there is snow on the ground. To remove the salty residue without damaging your vinyl or leather shoes, wash them with warm water and vinegar mixed in equal parts.

Afterwards polish with some olive oil and a few drops of lemon juice, using a clean sponge or rag. Leave for a few minutes; wipe and then buff up using a clean, dry rag or brush.

BURNED-ON FOOD
If you have left that burned-on food just a little too long without soaking, don't fear. Dampen the spots with a little water and then sprinkle liberally with some bicarbonate of soda. Leave to soak overnight and then use a non-scratch scourer to remove the rest. This works well on pieces of food that have burned on to the floor of the oven, too.

● **CARPETS**

Kids and pets can take a toll on your carpets and sometimes you need to freshen them up, especially in winter when you can't open all the windows. To give them a good clean, mix 125 ml (4 fl oz) of mild washing-up liquid in 500 ml (17 fl oz) of boiling water. Allow it to cool and mix well. Work a small area at a time using a damp sponge or cloth, rubbing gently in a circular motion. Rinse using a clean cloth and a solution of 500 ml (17 fl oz) of white vinegar and 1 litre (1¾ pints) of water. Wipe dry using another clean cloth.

For a heavy duty carpet cleaner, mix four tablespoons each of salt, borax, and vinegar into a paste. Rub the paste into the carpet and shut the room off for a few hours. When the paste is dry simply vacuum off.

To deodorize your carpets, sprinkle some bicarbonate of soda liberally on a dry carpet or rug and leave for around 15 minutes. Vacuum thoroughly and your carpets will take on a much fresher appearance and smell.

If you spill red wine on your carpet, soak as much of it up as you can with paper towels and then quickly pour white vinegar directly on the stain. Leave it to soak for a few minutes, then rinse it out with a clean cloth and water.

For fresh grease spots on carpets, sprinkle some cornflour on the mark and wait 15 to 30 minutes before vacuuming off.

● **CHOPPING BOARDS**

Simply rub a slice of lemon across the chopping board to disinfect the surface and get rid of any strong odours such as fish or onions.

● **COOKING APPLIANCES**

Coffee maker – fill the reservoir with a cup of white vinegar and top up with hot water. Run the coffee maker as if you were making a cup of coffee – obviously without any coffee beans – and once the cycle has finished, run it through twice more with just plain water. This will rinse out the vinegar and any residue that has built up inside.

Microwaves – microwaves are difficult to clean because you don't want to leave any smell behind that might penetrate the food. Put a plastic bowl three-quarters full with water in the microwave (make sure it is suitable for a microwave) with a few teaspoons of bicarbonate of soda and run on high for two minutes. Remove the bowl and wipe it clean with paper towel or a clean cloth. There will be no need to rub vigorously as every spot will come off with ease.

Ovens – how often have you used a harsh oven cleaner which has left you with burning eyes and a nasty feeling in the back of the throat from breathing in the toxic fumes. Make a paste out of equal parts of bicarbonate of soda and water and spread over all surfaces. Leave overnight and then just wipe it all clean with a damp cloth. Easy, and no caustic chemicals to damage your health.

Refrigerators – you wouldn't want to use anything perfumed or toxic in a place where you store food, so use the same paste as you did for cleaning the oven and use it as an abrasive to get rid of any stubborn marks. Wipe down with a clean cloth and water and your fridge will smell as fresh and clean as the day you bought it.

● **CLEANING METAL**

Aluminium – here's a handy tip if you have any old aluminium utensils that need a bit of a pick-me-up. Place two sticks of sliced rhubarb in 250 ml (8 fl oz) of water (or enough to submerge the items) in a large pan and simmer them for 30 minutes. Rinse the utensils in cool water and dry.

For larger items mix 500 ml (17 fl oz) of boiled water with 250 ml (8 fl oz) of white vinegar and 1 teaspoon of citrus oil. Leave the items to soak for at least an hour before rinsing them off and drying thoroughly.

WORD OF WARNING

Although aluminium does not rust or tarnish, it is highly reactive, and for that reason never use home-made cleaners such as bicarbonate of soda or washing soda.

Brass and copper – combine a few tablespoons of lemon juice with one tablespoon of bicarbonate of soda. Rub it over the metal and then polish off – hey presto, a beautiful shine.

If you haven't cleaned your brass or copper for a long time and it is heavily tarnished, you can soak it in hot vinegar and salt. Once you see the shine starting to show through, rinse it off in clean water and give it a final polish.

If you have stainless steel saucepans with copper bottoms and there is some burned-on residue, you can make a paste out of equal amounts of salt, flour, and vinegar, and gently rub on. Remember, never use steel wool or an abrasive cleaner on copper.

Chrome – you will probably find you have some chrome in most rooms in the house: in the kitchen, in appliances such as toasters, ovens, refrigerators, pedal bins, and taps and in the bathroom, taps on the sink and bath. Again, never use any abrasive cleaner on chrome as it can scratch or pit the surface which will never look shiny again. To clean chrome safely, apply either white vinegar or soda water with a soft cloth. Dry to a beautiful shine with a clean cloth.

If you want to remove burned-on grease from chrome, simply clean it with a few drops of undiluted eucalyptus oil and wipe dry with a clean cloth. Eucalyptus, although a natural substance, can be quite strong so wear rubber gloves when using it.

Pewter – wash pewter items in warm soapy water (remember though, only biodegradable soap) and then rinse with clean water. Polish with a clean, dry cloth.

Silver – Put some water in a saucepan and add a few teaspoons of washing soda. Bring the water to a gentle simmer, add a small piece of kitchen foil and then dip your silver into the liquid. Pull it out, dry it off, and then bring it to a shine with a clean, dry cloth.

Alternatively, you can make a paste with bicarbonate of soda and water and spread over the object. Use a toothbrush to get in any small crevices, then rinse and clean with a soft, dry cloth.

● **CLEANING FLOORS**

Before you polish your wooden floors you want to make sure they are really clean and you can do this by washing them with a mixture of warm water and white vinegar. A few drops in a bucket of water will be enough.

For sealed floors – use one part white vinegar to one part vegetable oil. Get a clean rag, soak it in the oil and then polish just the way you would a car. The end result is amazing.

For natural, unsealed floors – use pure linseed oil and work it in with a clean rag. Allow it to soak in for a little while and then repeat if necessary.

For vinyl and linoleum – Mix one cup of white vinegar with a few drops of baby oil to a gallon of warm water. For really tough cleaning jobs, add a little borax to the mixture.

● COFFEE AND TEA STAINS

If your cups are badly stained from tea and coffee, wipe the inside with white vinegar soaked into a sponge. For really difficult stains you can leave them to soak in vinegar for ten minutes.

To clean a teapot or coffee maker, add two cups of boiling water and two tablespoons of vinegar. Leave it to cool, wipe with a clean cloth, and rinse thoroughly with clean water.

● CRYSTAL DECANTER

If you have a crystal decanter that is a prized family heirloom, the easiest way to clean it is to fill it with fine chopped pieces of raw potato, add water and give it a good shake. Rinse well and it will be ready to take pride of place in the drinks cabinet.

● DISHWASHER

Rather than buying those overpriced dishwasher tablets, why not use equal parts of borax and washing soda. If your water is really hard then use extra washing soda to get your dishes sparkling.

To sanitize your dishwasher and remove any unwanted mineral deposits and smells, place lemon juice in the soap dispenser when the machine is empty of dishes and run it through your normal wash cycle.

● **DISINFECTANT**

For a natural disinfectant mix one teaspoon of tea tree oil to 1 litre of water to wash away germs.

● **DUSTERS**

Dusters will last much longer and work more efficiently if you soak new ones in a solution of one part water to one part glycerine. Allow them to dry thoroughly before using them for the first time.

● **FIREPLACE**

If, like me, you burn wood in your fireplace you will know how quickly soot and smoke smudges gather around the exterior areas. Make a paste out of cream of tartar and water and rub it into the stains. Leave it until it is dry and then scrub with clean water.

You can stop a build-up of soot in the chimney and fireplace by occasionally throwing a handful of salt into the fire. It will help to loosen the soot a little and give you a little more time before calling out the chimney sweep.

● **FREEZER**

If you have to put your freezer into storage for a while or it is not going to be used for a few weeks, then defrost it and wipe it out using a mixture of bicarbonate of soda and warm water to help keep it smelling fresh. Remember that you must keep the door propped open to allow air to circulate.

● **FRIDGE FRESHENER**

A quick and easy way to freshen your fridge is to soak a small piece of cottonwool or sponge in lemon juice and leave it on a shelf of the refrigerator overnight.

● **FRUIT STAINS**

These can be particularly difficult to remove, especially if you have dark purple stains on your shirt after picking blackberries. First plunge the fabric in cold water and leave to soak until no more colour is seeping from the stain. Next, stretch the fabric over a heatproof bowl using an elastic band to hold it in place and then pour very hot water over the stain with as much force as possible. As soon as you see the stain has almost gone, wash on as hot a setting as the fabric will stand.

If you get fruit stains on your fingers or hands, simply rub them in some vinegar or lemon juice and the stains will disappear.

● **FURNITURE POLISH**

Furniture polish is very easy to make and much safer for the environment than most of the aerosol sprays you can buy. You can make it as scented as you like and your wood will look like new. Try one of the three recipes below.

To hydrate old, dry wood
60 ml (2 fl oz) olive oil
2 tablespoons lemon juice
a few drops of pine essential oil

Use a clean lint-free cloth, and make sure you always rub in the direction of the grain. Work in until the wood has absorbed all the polish.

To clean wood
60 ml (2 fl oz) lemon juice
1 teaspoon olive oil
a few drops of essential lemon oil

Apply using a lint-free cloth until your wood is revived and clean.

For a general-purpose everyday furniture polish
750 ml (26 fl oz) water
4 tablespoons olive oil
2 tablespoons distilled white vinegar

Mix all the ingredients together and keep in a plastic spray bottle. Make sure you label it for future use and keep out of the reach of tiny fingers. Use a soft-bristled toothbrush to get into awkward corners or any pieces of intricate design on your wooden furniture.

● **GARAGE FLOOR**
If you have unsightly oil stains on your garage floor or drive, then you can scrub them with some bicarbonate of soda mixed with a little warm water.

● **GAS BURNERS**
If your gas burners are looking a little sad and you can remove them easily, soak them in a pan of boiling water containing four tablespoons of bicarbonate of soda for about ten minutes.

● **GLASS, MIRROR, AND WINDOW CLEANER**
If you want sparkling glass without too much hard work, mix white vinegar and water in equal quantities and keep in a spray bottle. Spray it on to your windows or mirrors, then dry with crumpled up newspapers; it works wonders.

● **GLASS SHARDS**
If you drop a glass and it shatters into a thousand small pieces, don't despair, simply put on some rubber gloves and cut off a slice

of fresh bread. Press the bread into the shards and the glass will stick into the bread easily and safely without any cut fingers.

● GROUT, MOULD, AND MILDEW CLEANER

If the grout in your bathroom or kitchen is starting to look a bit sorry for itself, take an old toothbrush dipped in vinegar or lemon juice and scrub between the tiles to remove mould and mildew.

You can also make a solution out of borax and white vinegar to spray directly on the mouldy spots.

● LIME DEPOSITS

To get rid of lime deposits inside a kettle, put 125 ml (4 fl oz) of white vinegar and two cups of water into the kettle and boil for a few minutes. Rinse well with fresh water while the kettle is still warm.

● MARKS ON WALLS

If your children have misbehaved and drawn on the wall instead of in their drawing books, pencil, crayon, or even felt-tip pen marks can be removed by gently rubbing the painted surface with bicarbonate of soda on a damp sponge. Rinse off with clean water.

● MOTHBALLS

I can still smell the mothballs my granny used in her drawers and wardrobes to stop her clothes getting ruined. It is a strong, chemical smell that comes from paradichlorobenzene, which is actually harmful to the liver and kidneys. Cedar oil will repel moths just as well and you can make pretty little sachets containing some cotton wool or fabric soaked in the oil. Alternatively, you can buy cedar chips and keep them in a small box in the base of your wardrobe.

Dried lemon peel also works well as a moth deterrent, so sprinkle some in your drawers and wardrobes to keep moths at bay.

Make your own moth-repelling sachets containing some lavender, rosemary and rose petals. These will leave your clothes smelling faintly perfumed.

● **NICOTINE STAINS**

If you haven't been able to kick the habit of smoking cigarettes and you want to get rid of those nasty yellow nicotine stains from your fingers, try rubbing your hands in lemon juice and gently work the stains off using a pumice stone.

● **PAINTBRUSH RESTORER**

How often have you left a paintbrush to go hard after a tiring day of decorating? If you soak them in some hot water that contains two tablespoons of vinegar and four tablespoons of bicarbonate of soda, you can revive ones that have been used for emulsion. Unfortunately this doesn't work on paintbrushes that have been used for gloss paint.

● **PAINT SMELLS**

I hate the smell of gloss paint when working indoors and I always make sure I have at least two dishes of vinegar in the room while I am working. The vinegar will absorb the odour of the paint, but remember to put fresh bowls out each day.

● **PEDAL BINS**

Kitchen bins can get very smelly and messy, so use a strong solution of bicarbonate of soda and warm water to wash them out. It is safe to use on both plastic and stainless steel bins.

● **REMOVING CANDLEWAX**

This is something that always happened when I was a child because granny had no electricity and we had to use candles to go to bed. Very often the wax dripped on the carpet, our clothing or the bedclothes, but granny had the answer. Remove as much of the wax as you can, then lay a piece of newspaper over the top of the wax and set an iron to low – you will have the advantage of a modern electric one no doubt! Once the iron is warm, slowly run the iron over the top of the newspaper above the wax. The wax will gradually melt and be absorbed by the newspaper.

If wax from brightly coloured candles drips onto a wooden surface, simply apply an ice cube to the wax to harden it. Gently scrape off as much wax as you can using a non-abrasive item. It may not be possible to get every single piece of wax off, especially if you are worried about damaging the surface of the wood. In this case get a soft, clean cloth and add a little beeswax to the area. Rub gently and the remainder of the wax residue should come away quite easily.

● **REMOVING FURNITURE DENTS FROM A CARPET**

How often do you move a piece of furniture and find you have unsightly dents in the carpet? I learned of this trick only recently and it really works. It is particularly useful if you are moving house, as you can guarantee that your furniture will not sit in the same place as that of the previous occupants. It's simple; just drop an ice cube in the dent and leave it overnight. As the ice cube melts the nap will begin to fluff up. In the morning you can mop up any excess water with some paper towel and the dent will be gone. If the dent is really stubborn you can always use a fork to help lift the pile after the water has dried.

● **REMOVING HARD WATER STAINS**

This is a hazard if you live in areas where it is very chalky – as I know only too well. Sprinkle bicarbonate of soda onto the stain, then wipe clean with vinegar. Get your children to watch it fizz!

● **REMOVING RUST**

Rust can be very difficult to remove, but did you know that all you need is some salt and a little lime juice. Sprinkle some salt on the rusty spot and then add a little lime juice on top of the salt. Leave it there for a few hours and then, using a small scrubbing or nail brush, work on the spot until the rust disappears. It won't take much effort, I promise.

● **REMOVING STAINS**

Stains will always be a problem, particularly if you are, like me, a messy eater. I always seem to have something spilled down my front, and very often it is greasy. If, say, your children have to wear white shirts to school, apply white vinegar or lemon juice to the stain. Allow it to soak into the fabric for about 15 minutes and then wash as normal.

If you spill wine on your clothes, put salt on the stain as quickly as possible. Leave it to absorb as much of the moisture as possible, then wash straight away.

For stains like red wine, chocolate, or any other dark marks that have been there for some time, soak the item of clothing in a bowl of glycerine. This is easy to get from your local grocery shop or natural produce shop. Soak the clothes for half an hour and then wash as normal.

Grass stains can be hard to get off, but if you soak the clothes in either glycerine or washing soda prior to washing, they should come out a treat.

For oil and grease stains, sprinkle some cornflour or bicarbonate of soda on the stain, then place the garment, stain side down, on a large rag on top of your ironing board. Iron with a hot iron on the wrong side of the stain and most of the oil and grease stains will come right out.

● STICKERS

If your children have fled the nest but have left nasty stickers on the bedroom wall where they hung their favourite posters, fear not, vinegar will do the trick. Simply sponge the area a few times with some vinegar, wait 15 minutes, then remove the stickers. This also works for stubborn price tags left on tools, kitchenware, etc.

● TOILET

Don't keep flushing bleach down the drain, use natural ingredients to clean your toilets, it will have just the same effect and you can rest assured you are not polluting the environment.

Mix together one cup of borax with either lemon juice or distilled white vinegar to make a fairly thick paste. Use this to clean the bowl and in all those hard to get places and leave it to do its work for about 15 minutes. Use a scouring sponge to remove any stubborn marks and then simply flush the toilet to reveal a fresh, clean bowl.

● UNBLOCK DRAINS

Put about one cup of bicarbonate of soda down the drain, followed by half a cup of vinegar. Make sure you put the plug in as the two components will react against each other and form a mini volcano.

Leave this concoction in the drain for about 30 minutes. While you are waiting for it to do its work, boil a kettle full of water. Then slowly pour the boiling water down the drain and it will take all the nasty residue with it.

● **UNCLOG THE SHOWERHEAD**

If, like me, you live in an area where the water is hard, you will find your showerheads quickly become clogged with limescale. Remove the head and fill a bowl with enough vinegar to cover the showerhead. Leave it for an hour or so and then run water through it at the sink for a few minutes.

● **UPHOLSTERY CLEANER**

If you have a constant flow of pets and children on your furniture, the upholstery can quickly look dull and sad. Make sure you vacuum it regularly but you can also make a shampoo to revive the fabric. Mix together six tablespoons of mild soap flakes and 500 ml (17 fl oz) of boiling water and whisk until you get suds. Use only the suds to clean the fabric, using a soft brush or clean cloth in a circular motion. Try to work only on a small area at a time and then wipe the soiled suds off with a clean, damp cloth.

● **WALLPAPER REMOVER**

To remove stubborn wallpaper, mix equal parts of white vinegar and hot water and apply with a sponge to help soften the adhesive.

● **WATER RINGS ON WOOD**

White rings on wood are the result of moisture that has been trapped underneath the surface. Try using some toothpaste or a little mayonnaise on a damp cloth and rubbing it into the ring. Once the ring has gone, shine with your homemade furniture polish.

Spring Cleaning

At the end of the winter I always feel the urge to rid my house and my brain of the numerous cobwebs that have gathered over the darker days. I can't wait to put on my rubber gloves and old clothes, and get down on my hands and knees and start spring cleaning. It somehow gives the home a sense of revival as you fling open all the windows to allow the cool spring air into the house. Modern houses are much easier to clean than in my granny's day when everything was covered with a fine soot from candles, fireplaces, lamp oils, and kerosene, which were used to heat and light the cottage during the winter months. When spring sunshine started to filter through the leaded-light windows, it showed up all the accumulation of winter dirt and the house had to be cleaned from top to bottom. Soot or no soot, it is still very satisfying and does the soul good to rid your home of winter grime.

Be careful though, it is very tempting to take a trip to the supermarket or hardware store and pick up every conceivable cleaning aid to help you in this task. It really isn't necessary and I am positive you will already have all the items you need. Cleaning without using any toxic chemicals is a wonderful way to turn your home into a healthy place to live for you and your family. Check in your cupboards and make sure you have the following items:

- A pair of sturdy rubber gloves so that you can put your hands into nice hot water without scalding them.

- A bucket for washing down paintwork and floors.

- Cleaning cloths and dusters. Disposable cloths are by far the most hygienic and they can still be washed out at the end of the spring clean and used again.

- A scrubbing brush. This is not essential, but if you have a floor that needs a really good scrub it could come in handy.

- A feather duster is invaluable for reaching those high places and for getting rid of sticky cobwebs.

- A good mop is essential for mopping floors, unless you are really old-fashioned and intend to get down on your hands and knees. That can be a bit back-breaking if you are not in the prime of life.

- And let's not forget our old friend the vacuum cleaner.

- Forget the bleaches, the aerosols, and harsh polishes – all you need are some lemons, a bottle of white vinegar, some bicarbonate of soda, some tea tree oil, and a box of borax.

- Buy a few houseplants to brighten up your rooms, as they help to detoxify the air.

At first the job of spring cleaning can seem a bit daunting, but if you break it down into separate rooms and make a checklist of the jobs to do, I think you will find it helps. Today there are numerous television programmes where a house is given a complete makeover, and in the back of your mind I am sure that is how you want your home to look when you have finished. There is no reason it can't be a home to be proud of again, once you have cleared it of all the winter clutter and organized your children's rooms into some sort of order.

The simplest way to do this is to take a notepad and jot down all the things that need doing in a particular room. Are there muddy shoes scattered all over the lobby, are there old books and magazines lying beside the sofa, are there too many winter coats hanging on the hooks in the hall, is there a pile of unworn clothes beside your daughter's bed – and so on? If you feel you need more room for outdoor shoes as you come in from the garden, make a note on the page that refers to that area and try and work out a solution. By doing this in every room, you could possibly come up with an answer for most of your problem areas.

Now, having made your lists, you can start with the actual spring cleaning. Remember, though, you will need to clear away or dispose of any clutter before you actually start as this will only get in the way and make your job much harder.

I usually allow a couple of hours to clean each room, although this is just a rough guideline and if you want to be really thorough it may well take you longer. If your eyesight is not as good as it used to be, make sure you are wearing your glasses, otherwise you will miss all the bits of food that the hand mixer threw at the wall in the kitchen or the bits of mould that have gathered in the corner of the shower.

Try to work systematically and make a tick list of everything you want to do. Start at the top and work down, making the floor the last job. Clear out cupboards, especially in the kitchen, where you might find that you have tins or packets of food that have gone out of date. Check the freezer, too; hopefully you will have dated all your food so you know exactly how long it has been in there. Make sure you dejunk your kitchen drawers as you will be surprised what you find in there. Take particular care of the cutlery drawer as this can gather dust and food particles.

When cleaning the bathroom, check the dates on any medicines in the bathroom cabinet and dispose of them if they are out of date. You wouldn't want to give your child some cough medicine that was supposed to be used up over a year ago! Make sure you give your shower curtain a good wash with a little vinegar in the water to help get rid of any built-up scum. When cleaning the toilet, use an old toothbrush to get into the hinges and any little places that you can't easily reach. Remember, a solution of tea tree oil and warm water makes a really good sanitizer. When cleaning your home office, go through the papers and shred any that are no longer needed. You might also like to spring clean the files on your computer as well; you will probably find that there are many you can get rid of or store on a back-up system to give you more memory to work with.

Children's bedrooms are usually a nightmare to spring-clean as they are normally full of clutter; that is unless you have the rare sort of child who likes to keep everything in order. I would not suggest throwing anything out without discussing it with them first, so it might be a good idea to get them to help you when it comes to cleaning their room. You do not want to incur the wrath of your teenager by recycling their favourite jumper or old Lego set! Once the room is clean and organized, try and work with your children to keep it that way by providing storage boxes or extra shelves for their toys and books. Suggest they colour coordinate their wardrobe as this makes it much easier when choosing an outfit – this works for adults as well, of course. Provide them with a shoe rack in the bottom of the wardrobe so that their shoes can be neatly put away instead of shoved underneath the bed.

If you are like me, you do not enter the shed or garage unless it is to get the car or the lawn mower out. In my view, they are the domain of the male in the household and spring cleaning these definitely comes under the category of BLUE JOB in my household.

When you are satisfied that you have done all your jobs and made a long list of repairs and other jobs you would like your DIY expert to tackle, then you might like to think about spring cleaning your garden, too!

NOTHING TOXIC!

I would like to finish this chapter with a recap on all the natural products you can use to spring-clean your house from top to bottom without once reaching for anything that has a warning label on the bottle. Many of the modern synthetic cleaning products are actually based on granny's original cleaners using natural products, simply because she got it right. Making your own non-toxic cleaning kit is very quick and simple, and will give you enough products to clean the whole house without running out. The added bonus is that they will cost you a fraction of the price, which means you will have more money to spend on something you really want.

Kitchen floors – If you have linoleum or ceramic tiles in the kitchen, a mixture of vinegar and warm water will get rid of all the grime. Use a good sturdy mop and get down on your hands and knees to get in all the corners or to clean the grout.

Kitchen sinks – Make your own safe scrubbing solution by mixing one part vinegar to four parts bicarbonate of soda and add a few drops of your favourite scented oil. Rub the paste all over the sink, taps, and draining board, allow it to sit for a few minutes, and then rinse off.

Windows – Good old vinegar again. Mix vinegar and water in a spray bottle to clean the windows. Wipe off using a piece of crumpled newspaper. Do not clean your windows if they are in direct sunlight, otherwise they will dry too fast and will become streaky.

Carpets – To freshen up carpets, shake some bicarbonate of soda over them before vacuuming, as it works wonders on absorbing odours. If you have any stains, rub some neat vinegar on them and then wash off with clean water.

Upholstery – Upholstery quickly takes on a musty, stale smell, so sprinkle with some bicarbonate of soda and leave for about 15 minutes before vacuuming off.

Mattresses – Turn regularly and sprinkle with bicarbonate of soda, leaving for 15 minutes to refresh before vacuuming off.

Room sprays – When you have finished cleaning, spray your rooms with a mixture of water and a few drops of scented oil. Remember, plants will help to keep your room fresh, and always open the windows when the weather allows.

Toilets – First spray with vinegar and then sprinkle on some bicarbonate of soda to make a natural, fizzy cleaning powder. Scrub clean with a sponge or brush and then rinse clean by flushing the toilet.

Dustbins and pedal bins – Sprinkle the bottom of rubbish bins with some borax powder. This will prevent mould and fungus from forming and is also great at keeping insects at bay.

Shower curtains – To remove mould from shower curtains put them in the washing machine with a few towels and a little white vinegar.

Ants – Spring sunshine brings all the little critters crawling out of their winter hideouts. If you are plagued with ants then you can keep them out of your kitchen by sprinkling a mixture of equal parts of borax and sugar at any likely entry points.

Ovens – Keep your oven smelling sweet by occasionally baking a few pieces of lemon or orange rind at 180°C/350°F/Gas mark 4 for about half an hour.

Sunlight – To protect your furniture keep it out of direct sunlight.

Chapter Two

Granny's
Laundry Logic

Washing Wonders

With soap in hand and water boiled
Granny grabbed the washing, soiled
She rubbed and rubbed until quite clean
She had no modern washing machine
When she was done, she pinned her hair
And with tea in hand, rocked in her chair.

With the wonders of modern washing machines, powerful stain-removing detergents, and many other labour-saving devices, doing laundry today is a piece of cake compared with say, 50 years ago. Visions of my granny bending over an old tin bathtub with a wooden washboard in one hand and a piece of homemade soap grasped tightly in the other, are still vivid to this day.

With no electricity or mains water, washday was a real chore for granny and, although the washboard was a godsend, it required a lot of elbow grease. Firstly granny needed to boil up some water on the top of her wood-burning stove to fill the tin bath and then, taking one garment at a time, she placed it against the washboard and rubbed it vigorously with a bar of soap. This had to be repeated until each item was washed and then the whole procedure of filling the bath with clean warm water started all over again. After rinsing each piece individually, my granny would put the garments through her mangle which, incidentally, had been handed down through a couple of generations. Once the laundry was drip dry she would hang it on the washing line, which ran the entire length of her garden. She was incredibly short in stature so reaching the line was not easy, but my grandfather had made a clothes prop to push the line high into the air once the task of hanging was complete. My granny would then stand back with satisfaction and watch her laundry blowing in the breeze.

Soap or Detergent?

Despite all the powerful new cleaning products on the market, have you ever stopped to wonder exactly what harm these chemicals are doing to your family's skin and, just as importantly, to our environment? Being a mother and a grandmother myself, I like to think that I care about the world my family are growing up in and over the years I have reverted back to many of the old tried and tested methods. These ways have been passed down from my granny, who actually wrote a journal about household timesavers. Although I am not suggesting that you buy an old washboard and do all your washing by hand, why not try some of the methods in this chapter to help get your washing clean and white without the use of any of the harsh products on the market.

Many detergents differ in their biodegradability and ingredients, so choose carefully as many can pollute the environment and wreak havoc for anyone with sensitive skin. The most common ingredients found in biological detergents are phosphorus enzymes, ammonia, naphthalene, phenol, sodium nitilotriacetate, and many other chemicals that the manufacturers don't even bother to list. These chemicals leave a residue on your clothes that is absorbed through the skin and can cause rashes, itching, allergies, sinus and other health problems. Health- and environment-conscious consumers are now opting for natural laundry detergents, so why not join them and choose one that is environmentally safe. That way you will be making a positive impact on trying to reduce pollution. Remember, everything that goes down the drain can have a diverse effect. For example, when phosphates were still used in detergents the resulting algae literally choked the life out of lakes and streams and killed off many freshwater fish. As tons and tons of detergent chemicals are used every year, our water supply becomes more and more polluted. Remember, natural soap is far less harmful than harsh detergents and can lead to less wear and tear on your clothing.

It is important to mention at this stage that you should always check the label inside any garment you are about to wash. The manufacturer will give you instructions regarding the correct water temperature, or whether they should be hand washed, etc., and these guidelines should be adhered to as I would not like to be responsible for shrinking or damaging your clothes.

Bicarbonate of Soda

Sadly, bicarbonate of soda is rarely used in the modern household. Its most famous property is probably its deodorizing action – it has an incredible ability to absorb odours and can neutralize them at the same time. It can also be used to neutralize acid spills on clothing, not only preventing damage to the fabric but also getting rid of the terrible smell of, say, vomit. The following are several invaluable hints and tips on ways to use bicarbonate of soda in your laundry.

Whiter whites – Add approximately four tablespoons of bicarbonate of soda to your wash when you add your regular soap powder. This will not only brighten your whites and make your colours appear brighter, it will also neutralize any odours as well.

Acid spills – Quickly rinse any acid spills and then apply dry bicarbonate of soda directly onto the fabric. If the acid has already dried on, then you can still neutralize it with bicarbonate of soda just before washing.

Coloured crayons – If you have accidentally washed an item of clothing which had a coloured crayon or crayons still in the pocket, then don't despair because bicarbonate of soda can come to your rescue. Simply rewash the clothing in the hottest water allowable for that fabric, adding half a box of bicarbonate of soda to the wash.

Ageing linens – Don't be disheartened if your old linen tablecloths and napkins are starting to lose their appeal. About four or five tablespoons of bicarbonate of soda added to the final rinse will soon have them looking as good as new.

Natural fabric softener – Instead of spending needless pennies (sorry, pounds these days) on fabric softener, try adding a few tablespoons of bicarbonate of soda or white vinegar to the final rinse. They act as natural fabric conditioners and you can have the satisfaction that they are far gentler than any proprietary brand for those people who have sensitive skin.

Cleaning the washing machine – Use a paste made out of bicarbonate of soda and water to wash the inside of your washing machine. You will be surprised just how quickly it removes built-up residue from inside the machine.

Luscious Lemons

Lemons come second on my list of things to use in the laundry. Lemon juice contains citric acid and, although this is quite mild, it has an amazing bleaching and deodorizing effect, as well as dissolving grease. It is an incredible stain remover which can be used on a whole host of different fabrics. When choosing a lemon for cleaning purposes, make sure it is firm and heavy with a fine-grained skin, as these are the ones that tend to have more juice.

There are so many benefits to using lemon juice in your laundry – it is chlorine-free; it is gentle on clothes and surfaces; it is a natural sanitizer; it is an effective whitener and stain remover; it doesn't give off any toxic fumes; it is both child- and pet-safe, and an added bonus is that it is inexpensive.

As a bleach – Regular bleach is a strong corrosive, which can irritate or burn the skin, eyes, and respiratory tract, whereas lemon juice is gentle and serves exactly the same purpose. If you wish to use lemons for their bleaching power, you simply need to lay the item of clothing out in the sunlight and soak the stained area with lemon juice. When the area is dry, the stain will have disappeared. If it is a stubborn stain then simply repeat the process.

If you wish to use lemon juice as a mild, stain-free bleach on delicate fabrics, then simply leave the clothes to soak in a mixture of lemon juice and bicarbonate of soda for at least half an hour before washing.

Underarm stains – If you wish to remove unsightly underarm stains from articles of clothing, then scrub the area using a mixture of equal parts lemon juice and water before washing.

Detergent boost – To remove rust and any other mineral discolorations from cottons, pour a cup of lemon juice into the washing machine during the wash cycle. The natural bleaching action of the lemon juice will quickly zap those stains and leave your clothes smelling fresh. This will also make your whites appear even whiter!

Mildew – If you find that the clothes you have put away for the season are stained with mildew, make a paste of lemon juice and salt and rub on the affected area. Leave the clothes out in sunlight to finish the bleaching effect.

White vinegar

Another item that you are certain to have in your cupboard, is white distilled vinegar. It is cheap, easily available, and harmless to use and yet it is a fantastic, all-purpose cleaner. Just like lemon juice, it is a mild acid so it is particularly effective on certain stains. It is great for removing limescale and calcium deposits – soap scum to you and me – and it will even unclog the washing machine for you. Simply pour one cup of white vinegar into the washing machine and let it run a normal cycle without any clothes. If you do this once a month, it should keep your washing machine free from deposits and hopefully alleviate the need for a plumber.

It is invaluable in the laundry, not only for removing stains but also for making those whites just a little bit whiter. Why don't you try some of these old favourites:

Prevent lint – to stop lint from clinging to your clothes, try adding half a cup of white distilled vinegar to your normal wash cycle.

Dingy dishcloths – If your white socks are looking a little grey and your dishcloths a little dingy, then add one cup of white distilled vinegar to a large pot of water and bring it to a rolling boil. Drop in your articles needing a facelift and leave to soak overnight.

Stain removal – Ketchup stains, or in fact anything that has a tomato sauce base, have always been difficult to remove. Try attacking the stain with a mixture of white distilled vinegar and water.

Smoky smells – If you live with a smoker, or you can't quite kick the habit yourself, then you will be aware that the smell of smoke lingers in fabric for a long time after the cigarette has been extinguished. If you are unable to wash the items then there is a simple solution. Fill your bathtub with very hot water and a cup of white distilled vinegar. Hang the affected garments above the steaming water, close the door, and leave so that the steam can penetrate the fibres.

Dirty collars and underarm stains – Spray the affected area with full-strength white distilled vinegar before washing.

Mouldy smells – Did you forget to take your washing out of the washing machine for a couple of days and it now smells mouldy? Don't fret, pour a few cups of distilled vinegar into the machine and wash the clothes in hot water. Then run a normal cycle with soap added.

Unclog the steam iron – To keep your steam iron free of mineral deposits in the steam vents and spray nozzle, fill the water chamber with a solution of equal parts white distilled vinegar and distilled water. Set it in an upright position and allow it to steam for about five minutes. When the iron is cool, rinse the tank with water, refill and shake water through the vents onto an old cloth. Test carefully before using to make sure all the vinegar has been washed out.

Cleaner laundry – To get your washing even cleaner, add a quarter of a cup of white distilled vinegar to the last rinse. This will not only remove the last remnants of soap, but prevents yellowing.

Refresh an ironing board – Spritz the ironing board cover with a mixture of white vinegar and water to freshen it up, and iron while it is still damp.

The Power of Sunlight

Although it is drummed into us about protecting ourselves from the sun to prevent skin cancer, did you know that our bodies actually need a certain amount of sun to absorb the healing vitamin D? In the same way, we can harness the power of the sun to help us with our laundry.

Too many people use a tumble dryer to dry their laundry these days. My granny was adamant that the line was the only way to get your clothes bright and smelling clean and I definitely agree with her. Natural sunlight is one of the best alternatives to harsh bleaches, and granny learned how to harness its powers. In fact, direct sunlight has one of the most powerful bleaching effects known. She wrote in her journal that it was invaluable for keeping her nappies white and, as a natural disinfectant, the sun also killed the odour that caused bacteria. I can honestly says that as a young child I failed to understand how this worked, but somehow it did.

If you have an article of clothing or household linen which has been badly stained, then wet the stained area and leave it outside in sunlight until it is dry. If the stain is being a little persistent then repeat the process until the stain has disappeared or use a little lemon juice to speed up the process.

Leaving objects out in the sun will also help reduce mould and mildew. It is a good idea to put bedding and items like cushions, loose covers, and pet bedding out in the sunshine to air from time to time. Even put your mattress out for a while, if you can find someone to help you move it, because this will make your bedroom smell much fresher and help repel any nasty bed bugs.

Manufacturer's Instructions

Are you confused sometimes by the manufacturer's labels regarding, washing, bleaching, drying, and ironing? You need to make sure you follow their guidelines to ensure you do not shrink or ruin your clothes. The symbols have now been standardized so that they are all universal, but if you are in any doubt, follow these simple guidelines.

WASHING SYMBOLS

 This symbol purely indicates a washing machine. The correct washing temperature is included inside the symbol, with a line underneath indicating a reduced cycle.

 This indicates a very hot (95°C) wash, maximum agitation, normal rinse and spin. This is normally used for white cotton and linen without any special finishes.

 This is the same as above but applies to a half-load capacity and only a short spin. Usually for white cottons and linens with delicate weaves that are prone to distortion.

 Hot (60°C) wash with maximum agitation, normal rinse and spin. For cotton, linen, and rayon items which are colour fast and have no special finishes.

 Hot (60°C) wash with cold rinse and a short spin or drip dry. For white nylon or white polyester/cotton mixes.

 Warm (40°C) wash with normal agitation, rinse and spin. For cotton, linen, and rayon where colours are fast at 40°C but not at 60°C.

This symbol also applies to a 40°C wash with reduced action for half-load capacity and short spin. Recommended for wool and wool mixes with cotton and rayon.

 Cool (30°C) wash with gentle machine action.

 Cool (30°C) wash for a half-load with short spin. Suggested for silk and printed acetate fabrics with colours not fast at 40°C.

 HAND WASH ONLY.

 DO NOT WASH

DRY CLEANING SYMBOLS

 If the symbol is a circle without any letter in the centre or a line underneath, this means the articles are suitable for cleaning in all normally available dry cleaning solvents. It is suitable for wool, cotton, rayon, linen, polyester, and nylon.

 This indicates that the fabric is stable in perchloroethylene and hydrocarbons (white spirit) without restriction. It is suitable for wool, cotton, rayon, linen, polyester, and nylon where restrictions on agitation are not indicated.

 This indicates that the fabric is stable in perchloroethylene and hydrocarbons but with restrictions on heat, water addition and agitation. Suitable for acrylics, polyester, and silks where weaves, surfaces or fibre mixes make the fabric sensitive to treatment.

(F) This indicates that the fabric is stable in hydrocarbons and spirit 113 using normal dry cleaning methods. For garments where surfaces, additions or materials are sensitive to cleaning solvents or heat.

(F) This indicates that the fabric is sensitive to normal cleaning solvents but has further restrictions regarding water addition, agitation, and heat. Any fabric that carries this symbol is very sensitive to both heat and movement and has to be cleaned in a bag.

⊗ If a garment bears this symbol it means DO NOT DRY CLEAN.

IRONING SYMBOLS

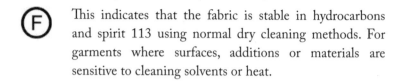 The iron symbol tells you that you can iron a garment safely, while the dots indicate the recommended temperature setting.

Hot iron (210°C maximum). Suitable for cotton, linen, viscose, and derivatives of viscose.

Warm iron (150°C maximum). Suitable for wool and polyester mixtures.

Cool iron (110°C maximum). Suitable for acrylic, nylon, acetates, and polyester.

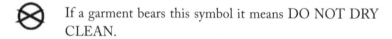 DO NOT IRON.

DRYING SYMBOLS

May be tumble dried at high heat. Suitable for cotton and linen.

May be tumble dried at medium temperature. Suitable for polyester, nylon, acetates, loose weave garments, and those with surface finishes.

DO NOT TUMBLE DRY. Applies to wool, acrylic, and most flocked polyesters.

Drip-dry. Suitable for soft polyesters and acrylics.

Dry in the shade only. Applies to cotton, linen, and any garment with vivid colours.

Dry flat. Applies to acrylics, cashmere, and loose stitch knitwear.

Line dry. This can apply to any type of fabric.

BLEACHING SYMBOLS

May be bleached in chlorine. Suitable for cotton, acrylic, and polyester.

DO NOT BLEACH. Applies to wool and silk.

Use a non-chlorine bleach. Applies to some wools and silks, and any fabric that can be bleached in chlorine.

Eliminate Washday Blues

Here are a few simple tips to make your washday trouble-free.

✓ Make orderly piles of washing according to their colour and the temperature at which they can be washed.

✓ Make sure none of the labels says DRY CLEAN ONLY.

✓ Check for any loose buttons and stitching or small tears in the seams. Repair before washing as the washing machine will only make the matter worse.

✓ Make sure you check all the pockets carefully; men are great at leaving some loose change in their pockets.

✓ Remove any fancy trims or belts that will not stand washing.

✓ Make sure any zips are closed before washing as an open zip not only puts a strain on the zip itself, but can easily rip another garment.

✓ Check garments for stains, particularly children's, and make sure you deal with these before garments are put in the washing machine.

✓ If you are washing delicates by hand, make sure you keep coloured items separate until they are completely dry, otherwise the colour will run.

✓ Soak any garments that are heavily soiled before putting in the washing machine to make sure you get the best results. Do not soak in very hot water as this can sometimes set the stain and make it difficult to remove.

✓ Check all the labels carefully before putting garments in the washing machine to make sure you are using the correct programme.

✓ Make sure you do not leave wet washing in the machine for too long, otherwise clothes develop a foul smell and will have to be washed all over again.

✓ Have a supply of plastic coat hangers ready to hang up any items that need to be drip-dried.

✓ If you have any items that need to be dried flat, then make sure you have a clean surface with a white towel over the surface to soak up the excess water.

✓ Make sure you wipe the washing line with a clean cloth before hanging your washing out, as it doesn't take long for a line to get dirty, especially if there has been a long period of wet weather.

✓ Turn bright colours inside out on a sunny day so that the colours do not fade.

✓ Any trousers with a pressed seam should be folded into the crease before hanging out as this will make ironing much easier.

✓ Never leave slightly damp washing in the washing basket. Make sure you either put it on an airer or into the airing cupboard to dry completely.

Take the Heat Out of Ironing

✔ Cotton or linen fabrics are easier to iron if they are slightly damp. If you have allowed them to get too dry, spray them with a little water first.

✔ Make sure you follow the manufacturer's guidelines on the label as to the correct heat setting.

✔ Do not use the iron until the indicator light goes out, otherwise you risk ironing at the wrong temperature.

✔ Make sure your ironing board cover is flat and clean and firmly secured. If you iron on a dirty surface the dirt can be transferred onto the garment you are pressing.

✔ If you have a difficult area to press, such as a jacket or dress sleeve, make a pad out of a clean towel and place it inside the garment.

✔ If you are ironing a pleat in a dress or skirt, or a seam down the front of a pair of trousers, make sure you always press it on the right side of the fabric. Place a piece of clean white fabric over the top of the crease to prevent the garment from becoming shiny.

✔ It is easier to iron the fiddly bits before the bulk of the garment, so that you don't risk creasing it again.

✔ If your garment has a lining, remember that the lining fabric usually requires a lower iron temperature.

✔ If you have a skirt or dress with a lot of pleats, it is easier to put large tacking stitches in first to keep them in place.

✓ Press collars and cuffs on the right side to make sure they are completely flat.

✓ Most important of all, make sure you keep the baseplate of your iron really clean.

Identifying Fabric Types

Fabrics come under two basic categories, natural and man-made fibres, both of which require quite different treatments when it comes to the laundry. The addition of prints, dyes, and different surface finishes can make a difference, too. If there are trims, linings, fastenings, tapes, and trimmings these all need to be taken into account, so the best and only advice is to make sure you read the manufacturer's labels regarding cleaning. Fabrics are not always easy to identify, so I thought it would be handy to give you a rough description of the main types of fabric you will come across.

NATURAL FIBRES

Cotton is an absorbent and hard-wearing fabric and is the principal clothing fibre used around the world. Cotton is cool, soft, and comfortable to wear, and because it is a natural hollow fibre it breathes and absorbs liquid easily. Because of its tendency to crease, manufacturers often blend it with synthetic fibres, which gives it better wash and wear properties. Today, many people are reverting back to wearing 100 per cent cotton, which can usually withstand repeated washing at high temperatures, depending, of course, on the finish and dyes used. The cotton fibre is taken from the seed pod of the cotton plant and, if looked at under a microscope, resembles a twisted ribbon. Because it is natural it can be bleached, boiled, sterilized, washed, and ironed at high temperatures without deterioration.

Linen has similar properties to cotton but has two to three times its strength. It is considered to be an elegant, durable, and a refined fabric which is often used for tablecloths and napkins as the fabric improves with washing and ironing and is completely lint-free. It is made from the stalk of the flax plant, which has a natural wax content giving it its fine lustre. This material can be dyed easily and the colour will not fade when washed. It does crease, but is much easier to iron than cotton and is strong enough to withstand boiling without damaging the fibre. Like cotton, linen is highly absorbent, but it has a poor elasticity and if used for clothing can wear quite quickly around the collars, cuffs, and hems.

Wool – this fabric is soft and warm to wear, but cannot withstand washing like cotton or linen. It requires careful laundering to avoid shrinkage, and the majority of manufacturers' labels suggest 'Hand Wash Only' for this reason. Some modern washing machines now have a wool programme, but you should still take care and read the label first. Some people find wool a little 'scratchy' when worn next to the skin and therefore tend to buy wool mixtures. Wool is dirt resistant, flame resistant, and, in many weaves, resistant to wear and tear. On top of that, it can absorb 30 per cent of its own weight in moisture before it actually feels damp. Wool is definitely the top choice for warmth and if you want that extra special feel you can always go for one of the speciality fibres such as:

Alpaca fleece is very rich and silky with considerable lustre. It comes from the alpaca which resembles a small llama.

Mohair is made from the angora goat and is a highly resilient and strong fibre. It is very soft, has a natural lustre, and is often used in home decorating fabrics and knitwear.

Angora wool comes from the angora rabbit. It is a very soft fibre which is often used in sweaters, mittens, and baby clothes.

Camel hair is from the extremely soft and fine fur from the undercoat of the camel. Camel is sometimes used alone, but it is most commonly combined with wool to make coats because of its exceptional warmth. Because of the natural beauty of the colours, camel fabric is usually left undyed.

Cashmere comes from the soft undercoat of the Kashmir goat. This is the most expensive of the wool fibres because it is a tedious job separating the soft fibres from the long, coarse topcoat. This very soft wool is often used to make fine garments and can be found blended with silk, cotton, or wool.

Silk – this is the fabric that conjures up luxury and sensuality. Silk is one of the oldest fibres known to man and for centuries has been associated with wealth. Silk garments are prized for their comfort and wearability as this fabric has an amazing ability to absorb moisture, making it cool in the summer and warm in the winter. It is easy to dye, retains its shape, and shimmers with a lustre that is unique. In the past, owning a silk garment was limited to members of the affluent society. Because it had to be dry cleaned, people tended to shy away from wearing anything made from silk. However, because it is a natural protein fibre, similar to human hair, which is taken from the cocoon of the silkworm, modern silks are now mostly washable. It needs to be treated carefully, and rolled in a towel when wet rather than wrung. Silk dries rapidly but should not be put in a tumble dryer as this can make it exceptionally static.

Hemp is currently coming back into vogue and many designers are now using this natural fabric, which comes from the stems of the

Cannabis sativa plant. It can be woven into a luxurious fabric which can withstand water better than any other textile. Hemp is very similar to linen in appearance and also creases quite badly, which has put many people off buying clothes made from this fibre.

MAN-MADE FIBRES

To try and improve upon natural plant and animal fibres, scientists came up with a range of manufactured fabrics, many of which start their lives as liquids. Many of these artificial fibres are exceptionally hard wearing and easy to deal with in the laundry, and today make up the mainstay of the clothing and fabric industry.

Acetate is often woven into fabrics to give them a luxurious look similar to silk, and is often used for evening dresses and light furnishing fabrics. It dries very fast and is resistant to shrinking, but you will need to take care if using natural acetate, as in nail varnish remover, as this could actually make your fabric disintegrate.

Acrylic is quite similar to wool in appearance. This is the first choice of people who seem to have an allergy to wool, as it can draw moisture away from the body, dries quickly, and is very light in weight. The drawback with acrylic, though, is that it will not tolerate heat.

Nylon is exceptionally light, very strong, and easy to care for. It is used in many household fabrics and clothing, and was the material of choice for the British army in 1942. The armed forces used it in parachutes, flak vests, and uniforms, but today we see it everywhere, especially in hosiery. It is not difficult to wash although whites should be washed separately, otherwise they tend to go grey. Also, when ironing you need to bear in mind that nylon will melt, so you will need to use a low temperature and always press on the wrong side.

Polyester is a strong fibre that is resistant to creasing and one which holds its shape. It is often blended with cotton to give it a permanent press property, but it must be remembered that polyester will melt if subjected to high temperatures.

Rayon is a natural cellulose fibre that has many of the qualities of cotton. It is strong, extremely absorbent, and comes in a variety of weights and qualities. Rayon can withstand much higher temperatures than polyester, but it can crease and may stretch when wet or shrink when washed, so take care when washing.

Spandex is a fibre with an elasticity that has proved invaluable in the making of foundation garments and hosiery. It can be stretched many times its length, and yet it will always spring back into shape. It is more resistant to washing, perspiration, and heat than latex, but you will still need to take care when washing your lingerie.

A Few Useful Hints and Tips

Odd socks!
If you keep finding odd socks at the bottom of your laundry basket, a simple tip is to join pairs at the toes using a safety pin before putting them in the washing machine. You will never have odd socks again.

Waste not want not
You know the little pieces of soap that get left in the soap dish that no one wants to use? Recycle them by adding a little glycerine and a little warm water. If you mash them up you will have a liquid soap that is gentle and economical.

Life back in old pillows
Are your pillows looking a bit sad and flat? To bring back the

fluffiness in bed pillows, put them in the tumble dryer; the warm air works wonders in just a few minutes.

Outside to middle
If you have bedsheets that are starting to wear in the middle but you love the colour and are loathe to throw them out, then simply sew the outside edges together and then cut down the middle and finish off the new side seams so they don't fray.

Washing red clothes
Why is it that red clothes always seem to run when washed? To stop this, soak the garment in vinegar before washing for the first time and you will find it works like a charm.

Tumble dryer tip
If you want to cut down on your drying time by as much as 30 to 40 per cent, then put two tennis balls in with the clothes. You will find your towels will be even softer and more fluffy than usual.

Chewing gum
If you find some chewing gum on your children's clothes, then brush on a little egg white with an old toothbrush. Leave for 15 minutes and then wash the items as normal.

Soiled collars
If you are fed up with trying to remove marks from shirt collars, try painting on some hair shampoo with a small paintbrush just before washing. Shampoo is designed to dissolve body oils.

Zips
To make a zip slide more smoothly, rub a bar of soap over the teeth.

Chapter Three

DIY

DIY
Survival

Do-It-Yourself

Armed with a hammer and some nails
Granny attempted to put up some rails
She sawed, she bashed, she tackled a screw
But still the damn thing looked awfully askew
Her face was red, so was her temper
And her body was covered in old distemper.

Another 'blue' job in our house, although I have to admit there have been many occasions when I have had a go. When I was living on my own for a spell many years ago, I felt I didn't want to call a handyman in every time a plug needed changing or the sink was blocked, so I enrolled in a two-day course at our local polytechnic. The little tips they gave me have been invaluable and, although I don't claim to be able to build a wardrobe, I am quite capable now of putting up some shelves that actually stay up and are level!

This chapter is designed to pass on the little tips that I have learned over the years, so that the next time you find you are on your own and a fuse blows or you need to hang a picture on the wall, you won't have to panic. Why not have a go, you'll be amazed at what you can achieve. Think of the money you'll save, and, of course, how impressed your family and friends will be.

My first suggestion would be to find out where the mains service meters are and how you can cut the supply if necessary. For example, where are your meters for electricity and gas? Are they on the outside wall? In which case you should have a key to enable you to take a reading. Or, in some older properties, they may be in a secluded place like a cupboard under the stairs. Find out exactly where the fuse box is, so that you won't be hunting round with a torch should something blow a fuse and leave you in darkness. The main gas tap is usually located near the pipe either in or close to the meter. By closing off this tap you are able to cut off the supply to the house, which is a good idea if you have an emergency, or suddenly discover an unexplicable smell of gas.

The main cold water pipe will come into the house underground, but there should be a stopcock in the kitchen where you can turn off the main supply. Most properties these days are attached to a main sewerage system and there should be an inspection cover outside the house. If you get an unexpected foul smell, it is worth lifting this cover to check the level of the problem. Older properties, usually in rural areas, may not have mains sewerage and get rid of their waste products through a septic tank. You will need to make sure this is emptied regularly, so always have the number of the sanitation company close to hand.

Always make sure you have the instruction leaflet on how to turn your central heating boiler on and off. Don't wait for a cold frosty morning to find out exactly where the pilot light and ignition button are; it is far better to acquaint yourself with these before an emergency.

The Toolkit

You probably won't have everything you need straight away, as a good toolkit builds up over the years, but there are a few essentials that no home should be without. You may have just moved into your first home and there are some things that need putting right, or you have decided to give your existing home a facelift. Your first job will be to put together a simple toolkit that has all you need for the usual household jobs. I am not talking about fancy spokeshaves or elaborate tools for woodworking, just the basic essentials.

Hammer

If you only have one hammer then I would suggest you buy a medium-sized one that is suitable for all tasks. Ideally though, your toolkit should contain a small one for knocking in things like small nails and tacks, and one that can cope with larger jobs. A good claw hammer is worth its weight in gold, as the claw side of the head can be used to pull out nails that haven't gone in quite right.

Screwdrivers

You can buy kits that have interchangeable heads which means you will have a screwdriver for every job. Make sure you buy a good quality one though, as some of the cheaper ones are much too flimsy and will break at the first sign of stress. There are two main types of screw head – one with a straight head and one with a cross which is often referred to as a Phillips screwdriver. If you know you are going to be doing a lot of DIY, I suggest you ask for a rechargeable electric screwdriver for your birthday or Christmas to make your DIY tasks so much easier.

Screws and nails, etc.

Keep these close to your hammer and screwdriver. Make sure you have a good selection of screws, nails, Rawlplugs, tacks, picture hangers, and washers so that you have something for every occasion.

Fuses and fuse wire

Make sure you keep these separate from the main toolkit, as they are items that you will need to find in an emergency. Fuses have a habit of blowing at the most inconvenient time. Keep a small torch with these items so that you aren't fumbling around in the dark. You will need fuse wire if you have to repair a fuse in your fuse box should you find that yours has short-circuited.

Pliers

You will need pliers for a multitude of tasks, such as pulling out nails, straightening out bent nails, or even pulling out old Rawlplugs from the wall. Try to buy a pair of pliers that has a wire stripper included, as you will find this useful if you come to changing a plug or putting a new plug on an electrical item.

Spanners

Spanners come in very handy, so make sure you have a set of different sized spanners in your toolkit. You will also need an adjustable spanner which is useful if you have any small plumbing jobs to attend to, such as changing a tap.

Allen keys

A set of Allen keys is essential for building many flatpack pieces of furniture. If you are moving house you might find you have to take apart beds, wardrobes, drawers, etc. and they are very often held together with bolts that need to be tightened or loosened with an Allen key.

Electric drill

You will probably find this is one of your most useful tools and is invaluable for hanging pictures, putting up curtain rails or shelves, or for any other task that requires a hole. Buy a good quality one with a set of assorted drill bits.

Saw

If you think you might like to have a go at putting up some shelves or doing some other simple woodwork job, then you will need to buy a couple of saws. There are many types to choose from so remember, a rip or cross-cut saw is one that cuts the wood across the grain and a tenon saw is one that cuts with the grain. You can buy small hacksaws with removable blades, or a panel saw which can deal with most jobs, but it is probably advisable to wait until you are actually embarking on a project before deciding which type to buy, or get some advice from your local hardware store.

Sandpaper

Make sure you keep a selection of different grades of sandpaper for jobs such as cleaning off old paint or smoothing wood.

Knife

No toolkit should be without a decent knife with a retractable blade. You will find you use it for all sorts of little jobs and it comes in very handy if you need to slit the covering on electric wires before stripping them back to rewire a plug.

Tools for painting

Have a selection of good quality paintbrushes, some masking tape, a bottle of brush cleaner, a roller and tray, and a paint kettle if you intend to mix different colours.

Wallpapering tools

If you intend to wallpaper then you will need large pasting brushes, a plumb line to make sure you get the sheets vertical, a large pair of paper scissors, a pasting table, some wallpaper paste, and something to mix it in.

Dust sheets

If you are not fortunate enough to be working in an empty room, then you will need some large dust sheets to cover everything over so that it doesn't get covered in paint or wallpaper paste. You can use old sheets or towels for this and remember, a jumble sale is a great place to pick up some bargains if you don't have enough.

Care of Your Tools

Having built up a good selection of tools, try not to develop bad habits and let them get into a poor condition. Make sure they are kept in a dry place so that rust does not blunt the edge of a saw blade or impair the hinges of your pliers. Make sure the blades are nice and sharp before you use them, as blunt ones mean that you will have to use more pressure and you stand more of a chance of slipping and hurting yourself. If you do let your tools get damp, wipe them down with an old towel and leave them in a warm place until they are thoroughly dry. Then coat them with either a lightweight oil or penetrating fluid, making sure you don't get any on the handles. Tools like chisels, that have to be extra sharp, can be protected by wrapping them in oiled cloths before you put them away.

It is also important to keep your toolkit neat and tidy so that you know exactly where a tool is when you need it. Keep the smaller items in a special toolbox or, if you have room, put some shelves up in your shed or garage and make sure you put everything back after you have finished with it.

A Useful DIY Guide

BASIC ELECTRICAL REPAIRS

How to change a fuse in a plug
If an electrical appliance stops working then the first thing you can check is whether the fuse has blown in the plug. Replacing a fuse is an easy DIY job. The fuse acts as a protective device that cuts off the electrical current if the circuit is overloaded or a fault develops within the system. It is very important that you replace a fuse with another of the correct rating for the appliance. As a general rule, use a 3 amp fuse for appliances up to 720 watts and a 13 amp fuse for appliances from

720 to 3000 watts. If you are in any doubt at all, check the instruction manual for the appliance or ask the manufacturer's advice.

1. Unplug the appliance from the socket.
2. Unscrew the retaining screw on the underside of the plug which you will find situated between the pins. Remove the cover and then lift out the fuse.
3. Choose the appropriate fuse for the appliance.
4. Replace the fuse in the holder and check that all the wires are securely held in their terminals and that they are in their correct position. There are three wires:
Brown – live   Blue – neutral   Green and yellow stripes – earth
5. Check that the flex is held firmly in place in its clamp.
6. Replace the cover with its retaining screw.

When you plug the appliance back in, it should now work. If there is still a problem, then there may be an underlying fault and the item should be returned to the manufacturer or taken to be repaired.

How to repair a house circuit fuse
The main fuse box is designed to distribute the electrical current to the various circuits in the house and each individual circuit is protected by passing it through a circuit fuse. If there is a fault or the circuit is overloaded the fuse will blow, warning you that there is a problem, and any lights or electrical appliances connected to that circuit will not work. Follow these simple steps:
1. Turn off the main power switch on the fuse box.
2. If your fuse box does not have a list indicating which fuse controls which circuit in your house, then pull the fuses out one by one and inspect them. Each fuse has a small length of wire, usually placed within a porcelain holder. It is usually easy to see if the wire has burnt through.

3. One you have identified the fuse, make sure that all the lights and appliances on that circuit are turned off.

4. Undo the screws at either end of the fuse and remove the old wire. Cut a new length of wire but make sure it has the same rating.

5. Thread the wire across the fuse, making sure you wind the ends around the screws and then screw them up tightly.

6. Trim off any excess wire and replace the fuse into its slot.

7. Switch the main power switch back on and make sure that any appliance or light on that circuit is now working. If the fuse blows again immediately, it is time to call out a qualified electrician to diagnose the fault.

Circuit-breakers

Some houses use circuit-breakers instead of fuses. There are two basic types – those with a switch and those with a push button. Turn off all appliances on the affected circuit. It is easy to identify which circuit-breaker has tripped as the switch will either have flipped to the 'off' position, or the little button will have popped out. Turn off the electricity at the mains switch before resetting the circuit-breaker, then turn it on again afterwards.

How to rewire a plug

It is not as difficult to rewire a plug as you might think and all you need is a small screwdriver and a sharp knife. Before you start, always make sure that the plug is disconnected from the socket and that the appliance is switched off. Never pull the flex to remove the plug from the socket, as this will loosen the wires inside.

1. Unscrew the plug cover and the grip that holds the cord, and loosen the small screws that hold the wires in place.

2. Make sure the wire from the appliance is in good condition and if you do not have sufficient length, strip off some of the outer plastic sheath using your knife to reveal about 4 cm (1½ in) of the insulated wires. Make sure you do not damage the outer covering on these wires.

3. You will now need to carefully strip the insulation from each of the inner wires to reveal about 1 cm (0.4 in) of bare wire, making sure you do not damage the wire in the process. Twist the strands of wire together, so that they form a good contact for each terminal.

4. Feed the cable under the grip and then take each of the core wires to their respective terminals. The terminal on the bottom right next to the fuse should be connected to the BROWN cable. The left-hand terminal should be connected to the BLUE cable. Finally, the top terminal should be connected to the GREEN and YELLOW cable. This can be a bit fiddly and you may have to lift or remove the fuse to gain access to the terminal. The terminals are usually marked in the socket casing with L for live, N for neutral, and E for earth.

5. Make sure the ends of the wire are neat and then feed them through the small hole underneath the screw or pin, making sure the wire has gone all the way through. Screw the pin down until it holds the wire firmly in place. Repeat for all three terminals.

6. Screw the clamp down to hold the cable firmly in place, otherwise you will find the wires work their way out of their terminals as you use the plug. Then replace the cover and screw in place.

You may find that some small appliances do not have an earth wire which means it is insulated and has no exposed metal parts. If this is the case, simply leave the earth terminal empty and just use the live and neutral wires.

Many new appliances come with a moulded plug which cannot be opened. I am afraid you will have to check with the appliance manufacturer if you need to replace one of these.

Changing a light bulb

I am sure you have heard the old joke about how many people it takes to change a light bulb. The answer is, of course, one, as long as you are careful and don't take any risks. Make sure the switch is turned to off and then allow the old bulb to cool down before attempting to remove it. Use a clean, dry cloth to remove the bulb just in case it is still hot. Never use a damp one as this could cause the glass to explode if it has not cooled down enough. Now insert the new bulb. If it has a bayonet fitting then you will need to locate the two pins into the slots on the light fitting and twist in a clockwise direction. If it has a screw fitting, simply screw clockwise until it is firmly in place. Remember, though, never try to force a bulb in place or overscrew it or you risk the bulb breaking. Now you can turn the electricity back on and you will have light.

Replacing a starter or fluorescent tube

If you have a fluorescent tube light and it is flickering or only the ends light up, this generally means that the starter is at fault and not the tube. The starter is a small, enclosed electrical component that fits into the end of the tube. If the light is dim or shimmering then this usually indicates that you will need to replace the whole tube.

1. Make sure your step ladder is sufficiently tall enough for you to reach the light comfortably. As the tubes can be quite long and difficult to manage, ask someone to help you and hold the ladder at the same time.
2. Turn the light off at the switch and leave time for the tube to cool down. To be on the safe side, switch off the light circuit by either removing the fuse from the circuit box or switching off the trip switch.
3. If it is the starter that is at fault, press the old one, then twist it anticlockwise (one quarter of a turn) and pull it out. To put the

new one in, press it and turn it clockwise to lock it in position. Switch the light circuit back on and check to see if the light now works.

4. If you need to replace the tube, unclip the diffuser (if fitted) and remove the tube by twisting it to allow the contact pins at each end of the tube to drop down through the grooves in the end support brackets. In some cases, it may be necessary to pull the ends of the fitting apart to actually get the tube out. Once one end is free the tube should be easy to pull out of the other end.

5. Fit the new tube in place by sliding the contact pins up through the grooves in the end support brackets and twisting it into place. Switch the light circuit back on and check to see if the light works.

Never put your old fluorescent tube out with your household rubbish as the dustmen will refuse to take it away. Always take old tubes to your local household recycling centre.

PLUMBING PROBLEMS

Bleeding a radiator

Bleeding a radiator is something you might have to do quite regularly. It is usually a sign that a radiator has a build-up of air pockets if it is not as hot at the top as it is at the bottom. What you need to do is open the air valve which can be found at the top of the radiator, and for this you will need a bleeding key which you can get from your friendly plumber or DIY store. Simply attach the key to the valve and turn until you hear a hissing sound – this is the air escaping. Hold a cloth underneath the key as you do this to catch any drips of water and be ready to turn it off quickly as soon as a steady flow of water starts to escape. Once the radiator is topped up, it should be an even heat all over and your system will now work more efficiently.

Dealing with a dripping tap

A tap that keeps dripping after it has been turned off, generally means that it needs a new washer. Not only is a dripping tap very annoying, it is also a waste of water so it is advisable to fix it as soon as possible. It is a very easy task and costs very little, so there really is no excuse.

You will need:
An adjustable spanner
A screwdriver
Some cloths
Wire wool
New washer of correct size (usually 1.3 cm/½ in)

1. Turn off the mains water supply. You should find the stopcock under or near your kitchen sink.
2. Now turn the tap on fully to drain all the water out of the pipes.
3. Just to be on the safe side put the plug in the plughole so you don't lose a precious washer down the outlet.
4. Loosen the screw that holds the handle in place, which should be located either on the top or the side of the tap. Then remove the handle.
5. Use an adjustable spanner to loosen the tap cover. Use a piece of cloth to protect the cover so that you do not damage it, and undo the large nut you will find inside the tap. If the nut is really stiff you can ask someone to put a spanner on the nut below the sink which holds the tap in place. This will hold the tap firmly and give you more leverage.
6. Then lift out the tap mechanism. You will see that there is a spindle that has a washer on its end. The washer is usually held in place by a small nut. Before replacing the washer, use some wire wool to clean off any corrosion and a cloth to wipe off any built-up grease

or gunk. Replace washer and reassemble the tap, then turn the water back on.

How to unblock a sink

I can't imagine that you have never had to deal with a blocked sink at some time or another, especially in the kitchen where greasy deposits can build up. If your water is taking a long time to drain away, take action before it gets any worse by using a solvent to deal with the build-up of debris. You can either use boiling water and washing soda or bicarbonate of soda and vinegar as recommended on page 29. Also make sure you regularly clear any debris that has gathered around the plughole, particularly in the bathroom where hair can easily cause a blockage. Next, cover the overflow with a cloth and then, using a plunger, make sure the plughole is completely covered and pump up and down several times. This works by removing and adding air to the pipe in order to dislodge anything that might be trapped in it.

If all the above fails, then you may have to be brave enough to dismantle the U-bend. This is the U-shaped pipe that runs below the sink where most of the debris settles. The U-bend has two sets of threads – one directly underneath the sink and one further along where the bend finishes. Place a bucket underneath the pipe to catch any water and then unscrew the first set of threads. Gently and slowly pull it free. Next undo the second set of threads, which will allow you to remove the whole section of U-shaped pipe. If there is a blockage, this is where it is likely to be. Use a piece of flexible wire and push it gently through the pipe to dislodge any debris. Then wash the pipe through with some very hot water and washing soda either outside or in the bath. Once you are satisfied that the pipe is clear of any blockage, replace it and screw the threads sufficiently to stop any leaks. Leave the bucket in place until you are certain there are no leaks.

How to unblock a toilet

There is something very disconcerting about having a toilet that is blocked, particularly if it is the only one in the house. It is very important to educate your family about what you can and cannot put down the toilet; after all, it is probably the most overworked piece of plumbing in your home. If your toilet is not flushing away properly and the water level seems particularly high, then the problem is usually due to a blockage in the pipe connected to the pan. You can buy special large plungers that cover the outlet entirely. Pump up and down several times to try and free the blockage and then flush the cistern several times. Sometimes, if the blockage isn't too severe, then pouring boiling water down the toilet can help to dislodge any clogged-up matter. If all else fails call your plumber who will check the drains to make sure you don't have a more serious problem.

Dealing with a cistern overflow

If you suddenly notice water running from your cistern or cold water tank overflow, it could indicate that you have a faulty ball valve. This is the valve that controls the amount of water entering the cistern. At a predetermined point the float reaches its highest level and then closes the valve to shut off the water supply to the cistern. If this is not functioning properly, the valve will not shut off and the excess water comes out of the overflow. Follow this simple procedure to replace the worn washer and your overflow problem should quickly dry up.

1. Shut off the water supply to the cistern and then flush the toilet until the cistern is empty.
2. Start by removing the end cap from the body of the valve; you might need to use a large pair of grips to do this.
3. Next remove the split pin on which the float arm pivots and remove the float arm from the valve body. The open ends of the pin will need to be squeezed together with a pair of pliers so that

the pin can be pulled through the holes in the body of the valve.

4. Grip the slide valve with your fingertips and pull out of the valve body. Depending on the age of your ball valve, the slider may be either brass or nylon – they are interchangeable. If the slider is brass you will need to unscrew the end cap, replace the washer inside, and then screw the end cap up again. If the slider is nylon, there are usually small slots on the end of the washer. Use a small screwdriver through one of the slots to help force the washer out and the new one is simply pushed back into the locating groove.

5. To reassemble the slide valve, simply reverse the above procedure, but there are a couple of points to remember:

(a) When fitting the slider into the end of the valve, make sure that the washer end goes in first and that the slot in the slider lines up with the slot in the body of the valve where the end of the float arm goes.

(b) After you replace the float arm and the split pin has been fitted, make sure you open up the split pin slightly so that it cannot be removed without the use of a tool.

IMPROVING YOUR HOME

How to put up a shelf

Putting up shelves is a fairly easy DIY job and it isn't difficult to achieve good results as long as you approach the task carefully. Whether you are using ready-made shelving which comes in flat-pack form, or starting from scratch, the main criterium will be to make them secure. Your first considerations will be the type of wall you will be fixing the shelf to, the weight of the shelf itself, and what you intend to put on it. If you intend to put the shelves on a partition wall, you will need to check that it is sufficiently thick to take the length of screw you intend to use. You really don't want it to come through the other side! Now follow these simple steps:

1. Make sure you choose brackets, screws, and Rawlplugs that are suitable for the size of shelf you wish to put on the wall.
2. Take the shelf and hold it up against the wall using a spirit level to make sure it is level.
3. Mark the position on the wall with a pencil where you would like the brackets to go. It might be a good idea to ask someone to help you at this point.
4. Remove the shelf and drill two holes for the first bracket and fit a Rawlplug into each hole. Screw the first bracket in place and then repeat on the other side for the second bracket.
5. Check that your shelf is level before tightening the screws completely.
6. Now secure your shelf to the brackets, making sure the brackets are equidistant from the edges; ideally the shelf should not project more than 2.5 cm (1 in) from its bracket supports.

Once you are certain that the shelf is fitted securely to the wall, you can put your favourite ornaments and books in place. Never overload shelves if you have any concerns about their stability, as this could be quite dangerous, especially if you have young children in the house.

How to put up tiles

I wouldn't suggest you try tiling a whole room at first, but if you have a small section in, say, the kitchen or bathroom that needs brightening up, here are a few useful tips. Tiling needs to be done methodically and carefully as it is possible to make a complete mess of it, but if you plan carefully and prepare the surface, it is a job that really can be quite enjoyable. For best results you need to put your tiles onto a clean, even surface, otherwise they will not line up properly and can end up looking quite messy. If your walls are really bad then you might like to consider having them reskimmed with plaster first. Once you are satisfied your walls are in good condition and you have chosen your tiles, you can get on with the task of sticking them to the wall.

1. Using a spirit level mark a true horizontal line at a low point on the wall – approximately three-quarters the height of a tile – and then lightly nail a straight timber batten to the wall. This will be your starting point and all the other tiles will line up with this guide.

2. Now measure the midpoint from each corner. You should start tiling from the centre of your batten and end at each side with a part-tile. You can either lay the tiles along the batten, or measure with a tape marking the centre point on the batten. When you are happy that you have it correct, you can apply the adhesive. Use an adhesive spreader that has grooves cut into the edge so that you end up with ridges of adhesive. Only apply small sections at a time and then place the tile in position and press firmly. Once you have completed the first row, the other rows should line up perfectly. You can buy specially made tile spacers to ensure you get your tiles evenly spaced along the wall.

3. Once your adhesive is completely dry, you will need to grout the spaces between the tiles. Make sure you force the grout into the spaces and wipe off any surplus from the surface before it gets too dry. Once the surplus is removed, run your finger or a grouting finisher down the gaps to get nice smooth lines.

4. When the grout is completely dry, polish the tiles to get rid of any powdery residue.

Cutting tiles

Of course in an ideal world, walls would be the exact length so that you never had to cut any tiles to make them fit. The cheapest and most basic method of cutting is to use a tile scribe and hand tile cutter. Mark the tile both sides where you want the line to be and then score down it using the scribe. Then use the tile cutter to break the tile in two down this line. If you have any fiddly bits to tile round, like a socket or pipe, then make a cardboard template first and use this to cut the shape out of the tile.

Decorating a room

Decorating can be very satisfying as it can quickly transform a tired-looking room into a vibrant living space. Preparation is probably the most important part of decorating and, although it can be a bit tedious, it will make all the difference to the finished job. Make sure you use good quality brushes, as the cheap ones will only leave streaks and leave hairs in the paintwork. I would also recommend using a good quality paint to get the best results. It covers much better than cheaper versions, does not streak, and, because you do not need so many coats, can work out the same price as using a lot of a cheaper brand.

Work your way carefully round the room filling in any cracks or holes with filler. Try and keep it as smooth as possible as this will save you a lot of sanding later. Make sure any paintwork that is peeling or flaking is either removed completely or sanded back to give you a good surface for the new paint to stick to.

If you have any old water stains a good tip is to paint over these using any oil-based undercoat, which you will have if you are intending to repaint the woodwork. Leave this to dry thoroughly before painting over with emulsion.

You can make life a lot easier by using low-tack masking tape to cover any areas that you do not want to get paint on, for example sockets, the edges of carpets, and glass in windows.

Now you are ready to start painting. Do the ceiling first, then undercoat the woodwork so it has time to dry, and finally put emulsion on the walls using a good quality roller. Cut into the corners and edges using a brush. Finish by giving a final gloss to the woodwork.

Give your curtains a wash and shampoo the carpet to bring it back to life. Now stand back and admire your work.

GUTTERS

It is very important to keep your gutters clear as it is their job to take rainwater from the roof and send it down to the drains. If the gutters are unable to do their job properly because they are blocked or cracked, then the water can run down the outside of the house and cause external damage and possibly damp internally. If you leave them too long, gutters can become full of old leaves and soil which will encourage plants to grow in them. This can stop the flow of water which will overflow over the edges and can cause a problem. You can help to prevent leaves from becoming stuck in the downpipes by placing a guard over the top or you can put mesh the whole length of the gutter. If your gutters are cracked, they can be temporarily repaired using a roof and gutter sealant, but ideally they should be replaced as soon as possible.

LOFT INSULATION

Insulating your loft is very important as you could be losing up to one third of your heat through your roof. Check your loft and see whether it has a good layer of insulation – the recommended thickness is 270 mm (10½ in). You may find your loft already has a layer of insulation, but if this has been down for a long time the chances are it is quite thin and you should consider replacing it. Some councils offer grants for loft insulation, so you might like to check this out first to help save yourself some money.

Loft insulation can be bought in large rolls that are easy to lay between the joists. Make sure you wear a dust mask and some gloves as you might find the lagging material can make your skin itch without some form of protection. Be careful to stand only on the joists themselves and not the gaps, or place some wooden sheets or planks across the joists to act as a temporary platform. If your roof space has gaps at the eaves, be careful not to block these as they are there to provide ventilation and to stop condensation forming.

Chapter Four

Safety in the Home

Safety in the Home

The carpet on the stairs was tattered and torn
Granny's old slippers were frayed and worn
The danger here was plain to see
And granny ended up in A and E.

We all like to think of our homes as safe havens, but a large number of accidents happen in and around the home every year. Falls, burns, scalds, poisoning, and cuts happen every day and mostly to children under the age of 15 or to elderly people who are not as agile as they used to be. Most of these accidents are preventable if we can make ourselves aware of the potential dangers and take the necessary precautions. Take time to walk round your house, going from room to room to see if you can identify any areas where there might be a problem and take action immediately. Use the following tick lists as a guideline.

HOW TO PREVENT FALLS

❏ Have handrails on both sides of stairs or steps, making sure they go from top to bottom.

❏ Make sure the lighting is bright over any stairs or steps.

❏ Make sure any small rugs are flat and taped securely to the floor as these can easily slide or cause people to trip.

❏ Keep stairs clear of any clutter.

❏ Have nightlights in the hall or landing so that people can see if they have to get up at night.

❏ Use a non-slip mat or pads in the bath and shower.

❏ Have a bathmat with a non-slip bottom to step onto as you get out of the bath or shower.

❏ Make sure your bathroom and kitchen floors are always dry and free from anything that can cause you to slip.

❏ If there are elderly people in your home, have grab bars in the bath and shower.

❏ Use safety gates at the top and bottom of the stairs when you have small children.

❏ If your windows can be opened easily, then put window guards on the upstairs windows to stop young children from falling out.

❏ If you have a play area in your garden with a swing, slide, etc, cover the ground surrounding the equipment with some safety material.

❏ Never leave any ladders around after use; store them safely in the shed or garage.

❏ Keep all patios and paths clear so that no one can trip.

❏ Fix any broken steps or paving slabs.

❏ Make sure there are no exposed wires or cables across the floor.

SAFETY IN THE BATHROOM

❏ Never leave young children unattended in the bath; always stay close enough to be able to touch them.

❏ Never allow the bathroom floor to become wet as some surfaces can become exceptionally slippery.

❏ Always test the water temperature before placing a baby or toddler in the bath.

❏ Never use electrical appliances in the bathroom. There should not be a socket or switch in the bathroom; a special shaver socket is the only type of power point for bathroom use. Use pull switches for lights or fixed heating appliances. Make sure any heating appliances are fixed high enough to be away from prying little fingers.

❏ Make sure any razors and razor blades are out of the reach of children.

❏ Keep all medicines, cosmetics, and cleaning materials locked away in a cabinet. Always keep them in their original containers with the labels intact, so that you know exactly what the ingredients are.

❏ If you like to take a relaxing bath using candles for lighting, always make sure you blow them out properly before leaving the bathroom.

❏ Keep any glass bottles or cosmetic jars away from the bath as they can easily slip through wet fingers.

SAFETY IN THE KITCHEN

❑ Because water and electricity do not mix, never use electrical appliances near water or with wet hands. Make sure all sockets are positioned away from the sink.

❑ Make sure curtains are at least 0.9 m (3 ft) away from the top of your stove.

❑ Never leave pans full of hot fat unattended.

❑ Make sure knives and other sharp objects are out of the reach of young children.

❑ Make sure all pan handles are turned backwards when in use on the top of the cooker.

❑ Keep your kitchen floor free of grease and water spills to avoid slipping.

❑ Make sure plastic bags are not within reach of children.

❑ Make sure flexes and electrical cables do not hang from the work surfaces as these can easily be pulled by young children.

❑ Keep a fire extinguisher and fire blanket in the kitchen.

❑ Make sure you keep a pair of thick oven gloves close to the cooker.

❑ Try to keep your kitchen clear of clutter, as working in congested areas can lead to accidents.

❏ If possible, try to use the back burners when young children are around.

❏ Remember, food cooked in a microwave can be exceptionally hot so always test it first before giving it to children.

❏ Keep pans, hot drinks, and baking trays away from the edge of the worktops so children cannot reach them.

❏ Do not use a tablecloth or placemats if you have toddlers as they can easily pull on these and get scalded by any hot liquids or food from the table.

❏ Turn the setting down on your water heater or boiler to a maximum of 49°C (120°F) to prevent scalding.

❏ Never climb on work surfaces to reach something in a top cupboard; keep a pair of small steps handy for this job.

❏ Always practise a high standard of hygiene anywhere that food is being prepared.

SAFETY IN THE BEDROOM

❏ If you use an electric blanket check the label and make sure it conforms to the current national standard. Make sure it is serviced and cleaned regularly.

❏ Do not allow your baby or toddler to have a pillow.

❏ Keep anything small out of reach of a child if it is able to stand up in the cot.

❑ If you are using a roller blind in the bedroom, then make sure there is no loop on the pull cord. Cut any loops in two pieces.

❑ Either fit a window guard or make sure the windows are locked.

❑ Make sure the cot is safe and secure, and the bars are spaced so that a young child cannot get its head through and become trapped.

❑ If your cot is second-hand, then it is a good idea to strip off all the original paint and repaint it using lead-free paint.

❑ When not in the room keep the drop side of the cot up and locked.

❑ Once your child can stand up in its cot, make sure you remove any mobile, or toys that hang across its bed.

❑ Make sure you keep any toiletries, lotions, and wipes out of your child's reach.

❑ Choose flame-resistant sleepwear.

❑ Make sure there are no pieces of furniture that can fall over on to the child and always remember to close drawers.

SAFETY IN THE GARDEN

❑ Avoid trip hazards such as loose paving stones, uneven surfaces, and hosepipes left unravelled.

❑ Never leave sharp tools lying around, always lock them away.

❑ Always empty paddling pools after children have finished playing with them.

❑ Learn which plants are poisonous so that you can keep young children and pets away from them.

❑ Do not use electrical equipment in wet weather.

❑ Make sure all chemicals such as weedkillers and insecticides are always locked out of harm's way.

❑ Never leave a barbecue unattended and make sure they are fully extinguished before going to bed.

❑ If you have a pond in the garden make sure it can be seen from the house. Put a fence around it to ensure that children cannot fall in accidentally.

❑ If you have to use a ladder remember to always face the front, don't overstretch yourself, and never leave tools on the platform at the top. Check that the ladder's feet are on solid ground before climbing and always keep one hand firmly on the ladder while working.

WEAR SAFE CLOTHES

❑ If you wear a full-length nightdress or dressing gown be careful when climbing stairs, especially if you are holding a tray carrying scalding hot cups of tea or coffee.

❑ Be careful of loose clothing when cooking as it can easily catch fire if it gets too close to the cooker.

❏ Remember that loose or flapping sleeves can get caught in door handles or on the edges of furniture.

❏ Make sure your slippers fit properly and have slip-proof bottoms. If you are not sure, remove them before going up or coming down the stairs to avoid falling.

❏ Make sure you wear proper shoes and not sandals when doing jobs like gardening or mowing the lawn.

❏ If you intend to use a chainsaw to cut wood, wear protective clothing and nothing loose. Also wear goggles, a face mask, gloves, and sensible shoes.

HOW TO AVOID A CHILD CHOKING

❏ Always cut a young child's food into small pieces.

❏ Make sure there are no small objects around your home that are small enough to swallow, such as coins, grapes, marbles, etc.

❏ Make sure your sewing box is not accessible to a young child as it can easily choke on buttons, safety pins, and other small items.

❏ Do not allow your child to play with a balloon unless it is supervised. If the balloon bursts and the child swallows a small piece, it can be very dangerous.

❏ Regularly inspect your child's toys to make sure there are no broken pieces that can lodge in its throat. Never allow it to play with anything that has small, removable parts such as car tyres. Always check the label to see if the toy is suitable for your child.

❏ Make sure your child's clothes do not have any drawstrings.

❏ Remove any jewellery from your child before it goes to bed.

❏ At Christmas make sure there are not any small ornaments on the tree that could be a hazard to a young child. Many toys will have button batteries, so make sure these are kept out of reach of toddlers.

WHAT TO DO IN CASE OF FIRE

❏ First and foremost make sure your fire alarm is working properly. Check it at least once a month and if it is over ten years old, now is the time to replace it with a new one.

❏ If the alarm goes off, make sure you get everyone out of the house as quickly as possible and then dial the emergency services.

❏ If you find you have to walk through smoke grab a towel (preferably wet) and wrap it around your face.

❏ If you are in a smoke-filled area, then crouch down or crawl along the floor as the smoke and hot air rise which means they will be less dense on the floor.

❏ On no account try to put the fire out yourself, as the fumes from burning furniture can be highly toxic and can kill you within minutes. Leave it to the experts.

Chapter Five

First Aid Tips

First Aid Tips

As you wait for the emergency doctor
Or perhaps the paramedics in a helicopter
Keep your cool and do your best
And don't stop the pressure on her chest.

Hopefully you won't ever have to deal with an emergency, but if you are in the unfortunate position of having to wait for the emergency services to arrive it might be handy to know what to do in the meantime. This section isn't about small cuts and grazes or the occasional headache but offers advice on how to stay calm in more serious situations. Try to take several deep breaths because panic will achieve nothing and could cost you valuable time. Once you have contacted the emergency services, they may ask you to stay on the line and give details of the patient's condition. They need to be able to understand what you are saying and, as time is crucial when administering emergency care, they will probably give you advice on how to deal with the situation.

No amount of knowledge or training can adequately prepare you for dealing with an emergency, and you will not know how you will react unless it actually happens to you personally. It has only happened to me once and although I did manage to remain calm and focused, once the paramedics arrived I fell apart completely. If this happens to you, at least you can feel secure in the knowledge that you did everything you possibly could to help the patient when they most needed you. Knowing how you can help someone in an emergency situation can help you save lives.

Every home should have their own first aid kit to deal with minor emergencies and although no two will be identical they should have all the basics you will need should something happen after the shops have closed. The list below is only a guide, but should cover most eventualities. Make sure that everyone in the household knows exactly where the first aid kit is kept, ensuring that it is locked away from very young children. It is also a good idea to teach your children how to phone the emergency services as soon as they are old enough to understand, just in case anything happens to you and there is no one else around. You should also have the number of your local doctor handy, particularly if you live in a rural area where it may take a while for the emergency services to reach you.

THE IDEAL FIRST AID KIT

- A first aid manual
- A good selection of plasters
- Adhesive tape
- Antiseptic cream
- Antiseptic wipes
- Calamine lotion
- Cough medicine
- Cream for bites and stings
- Eye bath and lotion
- Oil of cloves for toothache
- Painkillers for adults – such as paracetamol, aspirin, or ibuprofen
- Painkillers for children – such as Calpol
- Safety pins
- Sharp pair of scissors
- Sling
- Something for upset stomachs
- Sterile dressings and bandages
- Thermometer
- Tissues
- Tweezers

What would you do if you found a member of your family lying unconscious on the floor? Emergencies can happen to us all, but remember, try not to panic. When you stay calm, you make better decisions and will find it easier to remember the procedure to carry out before phoning the emergency services. If there is someone else in the house or a neighbour within shouting distance, attract their attention and get them to call for an ambulance immediately.

1. Check that the patient is breathing either by watching for movement in the chest or listening for any sound.
2. Check to make sure that the patient's airways are not obstructed and turn the head to one side. If it is an elderly person and they have dentures, make sure you remove these from the mouth.
3. Check to see if the patient has a pulse as this will indicate whether their heart is still beating. You can do this by using your fingers but not your thumb, as you could mistake your own pulse for that of the patient. Using the pads of three fingers, place them below the wrist creases at the base of the patient's thumb. Press lightly until you feel a pulse, if necessary moving your fingers around until you feel the slight beat. Alternatively, you can feel the pulse on the side of the neck by using your index and middle fingers in the hollow between the windpipe and the large muscle in the neck. Press lightly until you feel a pulse.
4. One you are happy that the patient is breathing and has a pulse, you should position them in the recovery position and then call the emergency services if you are on your own.

THE RECOVERY POSITION

In the case of a child over one year old or an adult, follow this procedure. By putting a patient in the recovery position you are making sure that their tongue is not blocking their airway. It also makes sure that any fluid, such as blood or vomit, can drain from the mouth. The patient is now in a safe position if you have to leave them on their own.

1. Kneel next to the patient and turn them onto their back.
2. Remove any jewellery or spectacles.
3. Next tilt their head backwards and push the chin up. Take the arm furthest from you and bring it across the front of their body. Then tuck the arm closest to you underneath their body.
4. Roll the patient towards you so that their body is lying on its side. Support the head as the body rolls and use your knees to help support the patient.
5. Bend the patient's legs so that they can support the patient on one side and make sure the chin is jutting out and the neck is arched so that their airways remain clear.

If you are dealing with a baby less than one year old, then you need to use a different method.

1. Cradle the baby in your arms with its head tilted downwards to stop it from choking on its own tongue or inhaling vomit.
2. Keep checking its vital signs until medical help arrives.

HOW TO TREAT SHOCK

The body's reaction to trauma is to go into a state of shock, which can cause the patient to collapse and leave them in a very weak condition. The signs to look out for include clammy, pale skin, confusion, disorientation, shaking or shivering, and general weakness, and you should do all you can for the shock victim while you wait for the medics to arrive.

1. Wrap the victim in a blanket to preserve their body temperature as you might find that the patient has an uncontrollable bout of shivering. A coat or jacket will do if there is nothing else handy.

2. Make sure you loosen any tight clothing such as belts, ties, or collars.

3. Lay the patient down with their feet elevated several inches above their heart to make sure their blood still circulates to all their vital organs.

4. Call professional help and then stay with the patient, trying to keep them as calm as possible. Hold their hand and let them know that you are going to stay with them as they will probably be very frightened.

5. Make the victim as comfortable as possible, but do not give them anything to drink. If they are very thirsty then you can moisten their lips with water.

HOW TO DEAL WITH CHOKING

If someone chokes on their food and is unable to speak, cough, or breathe properly, it usually indicates they have a severe obstruction in their throat. If the person is aged over one year, follow this procedure:

1. Using the heel of your hand, give four to five sharp blows between the shoulder blades.

2. Keep checking the mouth after each one and remove any obvious obstruction.

3. If the person has not expelled the obstruction, stand behind them and place a clenched fist between the navel and the bottom of the breastbone and pull inwards and upwards. Make sure you check the mouth after each attempt. If the obstruction still has not cleared, call 999 immediately.

4. Continue cycles of back blows and abdominal thrusts until medical help arrives.

If you are having to deal with a young baby who is choking you will need to keep calm and act quickly.

1. Lay the baby face down along your forearm, making sure their head is low and that you are supporting their head.

2. Using the heel of your hand give four to five sharp blows between the shoulder blades.

3. Stop after each slap to check if the blockage has cleared by checking inside the baby's mouth.

4. If the blockage still hasn't cleared then you may need to try some chest thrusts. Lie the baby along your forearm on their back, with their head low. Make sure you support their head and back with your arm.

5. Give up to five chest thrusts by using two fingers. Push inwards and upwards towards the baby's head against the breastbone, about one finger's breadth below the nipple line. After each thrust, check the baby's mouth to see if the obstruction has cleared.

6. If the obstruction does not clear, call 999 immediately.

GIVING THE KISS OF LIFE

If you have someone who has stopped breathing, you will need to take immediate action to try and save their life until medical help arrives.

1. Try to turn the patient so they are lying on their back. Tilt the head backwards so that their chin is pointing upwards.

2. Make sure they do not have any obstruction in their airways.

3. Pinch the nose between the thumb and forefinger of one hand.

4. Inhale deeply and then place your mouth over that of the patient, making sure that you cover it completely, and then blow out steadily. If the patient's chest rises, then you know that the air is reaching their lungs. If it does not rise, then it means the air passage is blocked, the head is in the wrong position, or you have not sealed the patient's mouth with your own.

5. Continue breathing into the patient's mouth in this way, checking

for a pulse after every fourth or fifth breath. Even if the heart has started to beat, do not stop giving mouth-to-mouth resuscitation until medical help arrives.

6. If you are unable to get the person breathing again, then you will need to administer heart compression and the kiss of life alternately. If there is someone there to help you, then you can apply both simultaneously until medical help arrives.

ADMINISTERING HEART COMPRESSION (CPR)

1. Lay the person on their back as for the kiss of life above, and then kneel over the top of their body.

2. Locate the breastbone in the middle of the chest and then move your hand along until you can feel the place where the lower ribs meet the breastbone. Then move your hand by about 2.5 to 3 cm (1 to 1½ in) upwards from the end of the breastbone.

3. Place the heel of your hand on the breastbone and cover this hand with the heel of your other hand, interlocking your fingers.

4. Keeping your elbows straight, lean down firmly on your hands to compress the chest by about 3 cm (1½ in). Release the pressure at once.

5. Chest compressions should be repeated at the rate of approximately 80 every minute and this can be estimated by saying out loud at a normal talking speed: ONE ONE THOUSAND, TWO ONE THOUSAND, THREE ONE THOUSAND. This will give you an approximate rate of one per second or 60 every minute, so by speeding up your speech you should arrive at the approximate speed required.

6. Continue to count out loud to help you keep the rhythm. Keep the compressions going until paramedics arrive on the scene. If there are others at the scene, take turns doing CPR so that you don't tire yourself out before help arrives.

Remember – the sooner you begin chest compressions combined with the kiss of life, the more likely it is that the victim will survive.

If you need to administer CPR to a young child, make the whole process faster and lighter by using two fingers instead of the heel of your hand.

HOW TO TREAT HEAVY BLEEDING

Would you know what to do if someone has an accident and they are bleeding severely? You need to stem the flow of blood, but first you should check whether there is anything embedded in the wound.

1. If the wound is clean, then cover the wound with a sterile dressing and apply pressure with your hand. Secure the pad in place with a tight bandage.
2. If the wound is on an arm or leg, raise the injured limb above the level of the heart to help stem the flow of blood.
3. If you suspect there is something embedded in the wound, take care not to press down on the object. Press either side and build up some sterile padding around it before bandaging, to avoid putting any pressure on the object itself.

If blood is spurting from the body it means that one of the main arteries has been cut and you need to take immediate action to try and stop the bleeding.

HOW TO TREAT A NOSEBLEED

1. Make sure the person is sitting down and ask them to tilt their head forwards to allow the blood to drain from the nostrils.
2. Get the patient to pinch the end of their nose and tell them to breathe through their mouth.
3. After ten minutes, ask them to release the pressure on their nose.

If the bleeding has not stopped, reapply the pressure for a further ten minutes. If the bleeding has not stopped after 30 minutes, then seek medical advice.

DEALING WITH A FRACTURE

If you are not sure whether the patient has a fracture or not, your main aim is to prevent further injury and to make sure the person stays calm and still until you can get them safely to hospital. If you suspect that the patient has a broken bone, follow these simple instructions:

1. Support the limb but do not attempt to move the patient. Try to support the injured limb with anything you have handy, such as a cushion or a rolled-up jacket.
2. If the injury is to the arm and you feel you can safely get the patient to move without further injuring themself, then get them to hospital as quickly as possible.
3. If you suspect a broken leg, a spinal or neck injury, make the patient as comfortable as possible without moving them and call 999.
4. Look for signs of shock and make sure you keep the person warm.

TREATING BURNS AND SCALDS

Burns and scalds are among the most common injuries that require emergency treatment, so it is worth knowing what to do should a member of your family burn themselves badly.

1. Your main priority is to cool the area as quickly as possible by placing the affected area under cold running water for at least ten minutes. Then cover the wound using a sterile dressing, making sure that it is not too fluffy, and call the emergency services.
2. While you are waiting for them to arrive you can raise the limb to try and reduce the possibility of swelling.

HOW TO RECOGNIZE A HEART ATTACK

A heart attack can be very life-threatening, so recognizing the signs quickly is important. The symptoms to look out for are:

• Blue lips
• Profuse sweating
• Extreme gasping for air
• Sudden fainting or dizziness
• A persistent, vice-like pain in the chest

If you suspect someone is having a heart attack, follow these simple steps:

1. Get the person to sit down.
2. Call for an ambulance immediately.
3. If the person is still conscious, ask them to chew on a 300 mg tablet of aspirin.

The main risk is that the heart will stop beating, so be prepared to resuscitate if necessary.

HOW TO TREAT ELECTROCUTION

If, for example, a child sticks its fingers in an electric socket, you will need to act quickly and calmly.

1. Dial 999 and ask for an ambulance.
2. Break the contact between the child and the electrical supply by switching off the current at the mains, provided you can reach it quickly and easily.
3. If you are unable to reach the mains, then you need to protect yourself by standing on some dry insulation material, such as a telephone directory.

4. Using something that does not conduct electricity, such as a wooden broom, try to push the child away from the electrical source.

5. Be prepared to resuscitate if the child has stopped breathing.

RECOGNIZING THE SIGNS OF A STROKE

A stroke happens when the blood supply to the brain is temporarily disrupted. It is important to act quickly as the longer the stroke victim is left, the more likelihood they will suffer from a long-term disability. Recognizing the signs is therefore very important, so look out for:

- Facial weakness – the person is unable to smile and their eye and/ or mouth is starting to droop.
- The person is unable to raise one arm.
- The person is unable to speak coherently and is finding it difficult to understand what you say.
- The person is complaining of dizziness and blurred vision.

Any of these signs and call the emergency services as quickly as possible, telling them you suspect the person is having a stroke.

ANAPHYLACTIC SHOCK

This severe allergic reaction can come on within seconds following, say, an insect sting or after eating certain foods such as peanuts. Common triggers include nuts, shellfish, eggs, wasp and bee stings, and certain medications. During an anaphylactic shock, chemicals are released into the bloodstream which can cause blood pressure to fall rapidly and air passages to narrow which results in breathing difficulties. The tongue and throat of the patient often swell to such an extent that they obstruct the person's airway. An anaphylactic shock can be fatal so you will need to seek medical help immediately.

Look out for the following signs:

• Anxiety
• Difficulty in breathing
• Blotchy, itchy or red skin
• Swollen face, neck, hands, or feet
• Swollen tongue and throat
• Puffy eyes
• Rapid pulse
• Abdominal pain, vomiting, and diarrhoea

1. Call the emergency services.
2. Check to see if the patient is carrying any medication. Some people who know that they have this condition always carry adrenaline (epinephrine) with them in the form of a pre-loaded syringe. Try to help the casualty to administer the medication or, **if you are trained to do so**, administer the injection yourself.
3. Finally, help the person into a position that can relieve any breathing difficulties.

DEALING WITH HYPOTHERMIA

Hypothermia is caused when the body has been exposed to the cold for a prolonged period and the person's temperature falls below 35°C (95°F). Although hypothermia is usually associated with being outdoors, elderly people and young children can suffer if left in poorly heated homes for too long. Elderly people who are thin and frail, must be supervised regularly to make sure they are eating properly and keeping their houses warm enough to avoid this condition. The signs to look out for are:

• Constant shivering and cold, pale skin
• Apathy and disorientation

- Shallow, slow breathing
- Slow and weakening pulse

1. Your aim is to get the person's body temperature up gradually. Cover them with a blanket and make sure their head is covered as well. Try to bring the temperature up within the room.
2. Give the patient a nice warm drink and some high-energy food such as chocolate.
3. Even if the patient is starting to recover, call 999, as it could be disguising the symptoms of a stroke or heart attack.
4. While waiting for the ambulance to arrive, keep checking the person's breathing, temperature, and levels of awareness.

If you would like to learn more about dealing with emergency situations, then I would fully recommend that you enrol in a first aid course. The British Red Cross or St John's Ambulance are always running courses, so you might like to contact them to get more details. They can give you tips on life-saving skills and give you the opportunity to learn how to respond to the most common accidents and situations. The more knowledge you glean, the calmer you will remain in emergency situations. This can be something that the whole family can become involved in as the courses are aimed at children as well, giving them the skills and confidence to know what to do if an accident happens.

Chapter Six

Kitchen Knowhow

Kitchen Knowhow

Granny put some cakes in the oven
And boiled some soup on the range
Grandad warmed his feet by the fire
And said something smelt rather strange
'Your socks are on fire, you silly old fool'
Cried granny, kicking away the stool.

Good quality cooking comes from the ingredients not the modern equipment available to young families these days. Yes, they certainly save time, but granny managed very well without a microwave, a juicer, a dishwasher, a mixer, or a toaster. She didn't simply open a packet and put it in the microwave for a couple of minutes, she worked hard and always put a tasty meal on the table. Stodgy puddings and potatoes roasted in duck or goose fat were not a problem as granny hardly ever sat down; she burned off most of the calories she ate. I can't remember ever seeing her with a spare tyre round her middle, in fact she was as thin as a rake. She walked everywhere, or got on her rusty old upright bike and cycled down to the post office or into the next village for a few essentials. She knew how to make the most of the cheaper cuts of meat, which used to melt in your mouth and tasted wonderful.

This chapter is not about recipes but about useful hints to help you make your kitchen work to your advantage. I have included a few useful conversion charts because I know I am always searching for one when I am using some of the old-fashioned recipes, or those sent to me by my American relatives. I have also included some tips on how to freeze certain foods and some useful suggestions about the microwave, if you feel you really must have one in your kitchen.

Smells evoke charming memories, like the aroma of freshly baked bread or a fresh batch of coffee on the stove. It is a powerful sense that can turn your house into a home. My children always say they love the smell of my home and that it always brings back happy memories of their childhood. It isn't a smell they can explain or one that I necessarily am aware of, that is until I return from a holiday and walk in my back door. Then I know exactly what they mean. I always have fresh herbs growing on my windowsill, cut flowers to freshen the air during the summer months, and no matter who calls at the house they will always be offered some cakes or biscuits that are kept stocked up for all eventualities. All these things add to the smell of a home. Next to my sink is a bowl of dried lavender and I always keep some lemons handy to get rid of lingering smells like fish, onion, or garlic that seem to overpower the other scents. My granny didn't have room for clutter as her kitchen was part of the lounge, so take a leaf out of her book and keep your kitchen worktops and windowsills as clear as possible. By doing this, not only do you have a nice area to work in, but you can keep it clean and hygienic without having to move a lot of stuff.

I learned to cook from my granny and mother who always had time to pass on their skills. Sadly, many modern parents are forced to go out to work and their lives are such a constant bustle they forget to give time to their families. Memories of standing on granny's old kitchen chair with my hands deep in a bowl of pastry, or helping her force sausagemeat into their skins, will never leave me. Remember, your children will have memories too, so why not make them happy ones that they can pass on to their children and grandchildren. Dig out some old recipe books and learn the real art of cooking and baking. Make use of your freezer to store homegrown produce and extra batches of delicious meals for when time is at a premium.

Oven Temperatures

CENTIGRADE	FAHRENHEIT	GAS MARK	HEAT
110	225	¼	Very cool
130	250	½	
140	275	1	Cool
150	300	2	
170	325	3	Moderate
180	350	4	
190	375	5	Moderately hot
200	400	6	
220	425	7	Hot
230	450	8	
240	475	9	Very hot

Metric / Imperial Conversions

MILLIMETRES (MM)	INCHES
3	⅛
6.25	¼
12.5	½
25	1
50	2
75	3
100	4
127	5
150	6
178	7
200	8
228	9
250	10

GRAMS	OZ/LB	
25 g	1 oz	
50 g	2 oz	
75 g	3 oz	
100 g	4 oz	(¼ lb)
125 g	5 oz	
175 g	6 oz	
200 g	7 oz	
225 g	8 oz	(½ lb)
250 g	9 oz	
275 g	10 oz	
300 g	11 oz	
350 g	12 oz	(¾ lb)
375 g	13 oz	
400 g	14 oz	
425 g	15 oz	
450 g	16 oz	(1 lb)
675 g	24 oz	(1½ lb)

Making Sense of US Cups and Spoons

Like me, you probably get very confused when American recipes refer to cups, teaspoons, and tablespoons, which all differ considerably to British ones. For example, a US cup holds 8.3 fluid ounces whereas a British standard cup holds 10 fluid ounces, so you can see it would make quite a difference to your recipe. Converting US cups into liquid measurements is easy if you are prepared to do a little calculating:

To convert US fl oz to British fl oz – multiply by 1.04
To convert US pints to British pints – multiply by 0.83

Other quick reference guides you might find useful are:

1 US cup = 8.3 fl oz or 237 ml
1 US tablespoon = 0.5 fl oz or 14.8 ml
1 US teaspoon = 0.17 fl oz or 4.9 ml

US CUPS	MILLILITRES (ML)
2 tbsp	30 ml
¼ cup	60 ml
½ cup	125 ml
1 cup	250 ml
1½ cups	375ml
2 cups (1 pint)	500 ml
4 cups (1 quart)	1 litre
1 gallon	4 litres

US OUNCES	METRIC GRAMS
½ ounce	15 grams
1 ounce	30 grams
3 ounces	85 grams
3¾ ounces	100 grams
4 ounces	115 grams
8 ounces	225 grams
12 ounces	340 grams
16 ounces (1 lb)	450 grams

Dry ingredients are usually measured in cups as well, but unfortunately this is not a simple conversion as it depends entirely on the ingredient you are using. As an example, a cup of brown sugar weighs 220 grams (8 oz), whereas a cup of plain white flour weighs only 125 grams (4 oz); this is why it is a good idea to get yourselves a set of US cups to get the quantity exactly right. Below is a guide for some of the main ingredients you will come across, but it is by no means a comprehensive list as this would go on for pages.

1 cup white flour	125 grams
1 cup wholewheat flour	120 grams
1 cup strong white flour	140 grams
1 cup rye flour	100 grams
1 cup white granulated sugar	200 grams
1 cup brown sugar	220 grams
1 cup icing sugar	120 grams
1 cup long-grain rice	185 grams
1 cup short-grain rice	200 grams
1 cup butter	225 grams
1 cup chopped nuts	150 grams
1 cup ground nuts	120 grams
1 cup fresh breadcrumbs	60 grams

Making the Most of your Microwave

Granny didn't have the luxury of a microwave and if she had she probably would have stood back and scratched her head in awe of such a machine. I would imagine most modern kitchens have one, but do you use yours to its full potential, or are you like many people who just use it for reheating, melting a bit of butter, reheating a cup of coffee that has gone cold or – heaven forbid – for cooking those TV dinners. If that is the case and you are not using your microwave for cooking, then you are missing out on a great cooking tool. Used properly you can produce delicious meals at a fraction of the cost because the microwave oven does not need preheating and cooks in a fraction of the time for conventional ovens. If you compared the cost of cooking in a microwave for 100 hours with that for a conventional oven, the energy the microwave would use would cost around £4 and the conventional oven around £40, so you can see how much money you could save in a year.

Some of my friends and family seem cautious over the safety of microwaves, so understanding exactly how they work could possibly alleviate some of these fears. The microwaves produced in the oven are attracted to the molecules of fat, sugar, and water within the food itself. These microwaves reflect against the metal walls of the oven so that the molecules start to vibrate against one another. This causes friction and it is this friction which actually produces the heat to cook the food. Because the microwaves can only penetrate 25–38 mm (1–1½ in) into the surface of the food, it is important to use the right size dish and the food should be spread evenly within the dish. Microwaves can pass through plastic, wood, paper, and glass but not metal. That is why you should never put anything metal into a microwave, otherwise you will cause 'arcing' or sparking which could lead to a fire or explosion.

Here are some general rules to follow when cooking in a microwave:

• Because microwave cooking does not evaporate so much moisture from the food, you need to reduce the liquid specified in your recipe by one quarter.

• To ensure even cooking, arrange the thicker part of your food on the outside and the thinner part inside.

• Microwave cooking increases the flavour of herbs and spices, so reduce the amount you would normally use by half.

- Any foods containing liquid, sugar, and fat cook faster in a microwave than in a conventional oven. Start off by reducing the cooking time by one quarter of conventional cooking and then gradually increase it until you get the desired result.

- Cut the amount of salt by one third as microwave cooking enhances the flavour. You can always add salt after the food is cooked if you feel there is not enough.

- Keep the inside of your microwave clean by using about a tablespoon of bicarbonate of soda in a microwave-safe bowl half-filled with water. Microwave for about three minutes ONLY and you will find any splatters simply wipe off.

- Never microwave any dishes that are covered with aluminium foil.

- Add cheese and other similar toppings near the end of the cooking time, otherwise you risk the top becoming tough or soggy.

- Always make sure there is room for the steam to escape if you are covering a dish.

- The general rule of thumb is to allow six minutes for every pound of food, with the exception of seafood which doesn't require as long.

- Remember that 20 per cent of the cooking takes place after the oven is turned off, so you will need to make allowance for this.

- If you wish to convert your conventional oven temperatures to those of your microwave, remember a microwave used on HIGH or 100 per cent of its power is about the same as having your conventional oven at 220°C/425°F/gas mark 7. A 180°C/350°F/

gas mark 4 oven would be equivalent to using a microwave at 50 per cent of its power.

- A quick way of assessing your microwave's wattage is to place one cupful of water in a jug. Heat the water on high for two minutes and if it boils in two minutes or less, the microwave is probably 700 watts or more. If it takes longer then it is probably 600 watts or less.

- Using a dish with a cone in the middle can help to distribute the heat evenly.

- When baking cakes, or any food that contains baking powder, allow the mixture to stand for a few minutes before cooking to give the rising agents time to work.

- Remember, food that has been cooked in a microwave will be exceptionally hot, so always open covers away from you to release the steam.

- Any food that has a skin or membrane must be pricked before cooking in a microwave. If you don't do this, the build-up of heat within the food may cause it to burst.

- During microwave cooking it is important to stir or rearrange food to ensure that it is cooked evenly.

- Onions and garlic need to be cooked first, otherwise you might find their flavour is too overpowering.

- When heating cream or sour cream, set the heat to 50 per cent to avoid curdling.

• Never cook eggs in their shells as they are liable to explode.

• If you want to soften hard-packed brown sugar, put it in a microwavable bowl with a slice of apple or fresh bread, cover with clingfilm and heat on high for about 30 seconds.

• If you want to make breadcrumbs in a hurry, cut some bread up into cubes and microwave on high until they become hard. Crush the cubes in a resealable plastic bag.

• If your honey has gone hard, put it in a microwavable jug, cover with clingfilm, making sure you leave space for the steam to escape, then microwave for approximately one minute.

• To dry orange and lemon peel, place grated rind in a container that is suitable for the microwave and heat on high power for about 30 to 60 seconds.

• To get more juice out of citrus fruit, microwave for about 20 seconds and then roll it on a worktop before cutting and extracting the juice.

• To make dried fruit plump again, take about a cup of fruit and sprinkle with a couple of tablespoons of water. Cover loosely with clingfilm and then heat on high for about 30 seconds.

• If you want to dry herbs quickly, spread them into a single layer between some paper towels. Heat on full power for approximately two to three minutes. After the first minute, start to check the herbs at half-minute intervals. When the herbs are dry, crumble and store in airtight containers.

- If you have some crisps or biscuits that have gone a bit soft, microwave them on full power for about ten seconds.

- A quick way to blanch nuts is to put them in some boiling water and heat on high for one minute. Remove the skins by rubbing between some kitchen paper.

- You can quickly roast nuts by spreading them evenly in a single layer and cooking on high for 2½ to 3 minutes.

- To make light, fluffy mashed potato in the microwave, cut potatoes into small pieces and place in a microwavable container with one to two tablespoons of water. Cover with plastic wrap, making sure you leave a small space for the steam to escape. Microwave on high until soft and then mash with milk, butter, and seasoning to taste.

- If you want to bake a whole potato in the microwave, make sure you pierce the skin first to release the steam.

- If you want to cook corn on the cob in the microwave, rinse under cold water with the husks still on and then heat in the microwave on high for about six minutes (for two cobs).

- Melting chocolate in a microwave is simple and does away with the need for a double boiler. Microwave it at medium for 2½ minutes.

- Check that food is piping hot before serving and if it is not hot enough, return to oven for further reheating.

- Foods not suitable for cooking by microwave include Yorkshire puddings, soufflés, and pastry.

Tips on Using a Pressure Cooker

I have to admit I always thought pressure cookers were 'dangerous' until an elderly aunt gave me one as a Christmas present. It sat in the box for several months until I was actually brave enough to get the leaflet out and read about it. Today I wouldn't be without it and I have turned out many delicious casseroles, roasts and stews in half the time. Many busy housewives are returning to the old ways of cooking using a pressure cooker as a way of creating healthy meals without losing any of the nutrients. As long as they are used in accordance with the manufacturer's instructions, nothing should go wrong and you can cut your cooking time by hours.

So how does a pressure cooker work? It is a sealed pot that heats the water or other liquid to a temperature of about 120°C (248°F), which is a far higher temperature than can be reached by ordinary boiling. As the temperature of the water in the pressure cooker rises, some of the water changes to steam causing a mixture of steam and air to be released via a safety valve. Once all the air is released, pressure starts to build up inside the pot. When the correct amount of pressure is reached, the heat is turned down to a level where the pressure can be maintained. In modern pressure cookers, the safety valve has a back-up system in case the pressure valve becomes clogged in any way. The foods that cause the most problems with foaming include split peas and beans, oatmeal, apples, cranberries, rhubarb, pasta, and pearl barley, so it is probably best to avoid these.

If you have one of the older-style pressure cookers, the steam has to be released by placing the cooker in the sink and running cold water over it, making sure you keep the water out of the steam valve. You need to release the steam from the pressure cooker before you can open the lid, so it is important that you let the cooker cool down.

Timing is crucial when using a pressure cooker, and I would recommend you undercook rather than overcook, until you get the timing right. If your pressure cooker doesn't have a built-in timer, then go out and get yourself an accurate timer that you can use every time you cook by this method. The booklet that comes with your cooker should give you guidelines on cooking times.

Follow these safety precautions:

- Never fill a pressure cooker more than two-thirds full. If you are cooking foods that are going to expand, like rice or dried vegetables, only fill the pressure cooker half-full.

- Never open the pressure cooker until it has cooled and the inside pressure has been reduced.

- Never open the pressure cooker towards your face, even if you have released the steam.

- Make sure you regularly inspect the rubber ring to make sure it is still flexible, otherwise you will not be able to achieve a good seal.

- Always check to make sure the valves are absolutely clean and free from any food before using your pressure cooker.

- Never use your pressure cooker as a deep fat fryer.

- Never use oil or fat only as it cannot produce enough steam.

- Never leave your pressure cooker unattended for any length of time.

- Always make sure you include enough liquid to build up pressure; the minimum amount is usually about 300 ml (10 fl oz).

- Be careful with seasoning when cooking in a pressure cooker because the flavours tend to become more concentrated.

- You can achieve extra flavour in your food if you brown foods like meat and onions before adding them to the pressure cooker.

There are two ways of releasing the pressure from a pressure cooker, but this will depend upon the type of cooker you have and what you are intending to cook.

The Natural (or Slow) Release Method

This is suitable for stocks, soups containing beans or pasta, cereals, pulses, and stews that are made with tougher cuts of meat. Simply take the pan off the heat and leave until the pressure has dropped. This takes anywhere from 10 to 15 minutes.

Quick Release Method

This is suitable for soups, fish, poultry, and vegetables that do not require such long cooking times. Some pressure cookers will have an automatic release method, so make sure you check the manufacturer's instructions first. If yours is the type that doesn't, simply transfer the cooker to the sink and run cold water over the top until the pressure is released. This generally takes a couple of minutes.

Most recipes can be adapted for cooking in a pressure cooker as long as there is enough liquid to create steam. Follow the recipe up to the point where the liquid is added. Make sure you add vegetables and potatoes later in the cooking stage, otherwise you risk them turning to mush. If you want to cook pulses, then be sure to soak them in boiling water for at least an hour before adding to the pressure cooker. As a rough guideline, you can reduce the cooking time by about two-thirds.

Granny's Beef Stew

To this day I can taste the succulent beef that literally melted in your mouth. Nothing can beat it on a cold winter's night and it doesn't take hours to cook either.

You will need

1 tablespoon olive oil
1 small onion, diced
1 kg stewing beef, cubed
225 ml (8 fl oz) beef stock
225 ml (8 fl oz) water

5 carrots, peeled and diced
salt to taste
1 dessertspoon cornflour
8 medium potatoes, peeled
 and diced

Method

1. Heat the oil in the bottom of the pressure cooker over medium high heat. Add the onion and beef and cook until browned on the outside.

2. Stir in the stock, water, carrots, and salt, close the lid and secure the pressure regulator. Heat until you start to hear sizzling and then reduce the heat to medium. Set your timer for 20 minutes. If you have an adjustable pressure regulator, set it for 10 pounds of pressure.

3. Meanwhile cook the potatoes and drain.

4. When the 20 minutes are up, release the pressure from the cooker according to the manufacturer's instructions.

5. Remove the lid, and place the pot over medium heat. Bring to the boil. Stir the cornflour into a small amount of cold water until it has dissolved. Stir this into the stew and cook for a few minutes.

6. Add the potatoes to the stew or place them in serving dishes. Ladle the stew over them and enjoy.

Freezer Freedom

Freezing is a wonderful way of preserving food without losing the quality and nutrients of the original product. It means you can cook less often, shop less often, and give yourself more time to do things you really enjoy. By cooking in quantity and freezing in portions, it means you will never get caught short if that unexpected guest arrives for dinner. Both fresh and cooked foods can be stored for weeks and sometimes months, and this section gives you tips on how to freeze successfully. Not all foods are suitable for home freezing, but the majority are and I am including a chart to advise you on the best way to go about it.

First of all, follow these tips to make the most out of your freezer:

- Make sure your freezer is below 0°F (−18°C) and be sure to check it regularly using a thermometer.

- Always freeze in small portions so the food not only freezes more quickly, but defrosts faster for best quality. You also eliminate waste as you may not always want to use a large quantity.

- Make sure you always label your cartons or freezer bags, including the date it was frozen and what the content is.

- Only freeze top quality food, as freezing will only keep it at its original freshness.

- Make sure the foods are well wrapped, otherwise you risk getting freezer burn caused by improper packing.

- Leave space around newly introduced freezer packages.

- Always leave items to defrost in the refrigerator or in cold water if you are in a hurry.

How does freezing work?

Fresh food contains a high quantity of water and freezing the water molecules helps to prevent the growth of micro-organisms and bacteria. The secret to maintaining freshness and quality in your food is to freeze it as fast as possible. If you have a 'fast freeze' option in your freezer then use this, or alternatively place it in the coldest area which is the bottom of the freezer. If you are freezing several items at the same time, make sure you give them plenty of space until they have frozen, otherwise they will take longer to freeze. The ideal temperature to store food is at 0°F (−18°C), anything higher than this and the food will start to deteriorate as it will be prone to bacteria.

Because freezing does not destroy the bacteria present in food, it is important to thaw slowly and in cool temperatures. If you leave frozen food out at room temperature, the bacteria will start to grow in the moisture and you risk giving members of your family food poisoning or at least a nasty stomach upset. The ideal way to defrost food is to leave it in the refrigerator overnight.

Ideally, food should be frozen on the day it was bought or the day it was picked if you are getting it from your own garden. Freezing will not destroy the nutritional value of the food, in fact it will maintain its goodness for far longer than foods that are just left to stand on a shelf. Fruit and vegetables will actually begin to lose many of their vitamins and minerals shortly after picking, so freezing them quickly can retain their fresh-picked quality. Meat, fish, and poultry lose hardly any nutrients at all by freezing, so you can be sure you are not destroying any of their original goodness.

Blanching

Vegetables generally need to be blanched – or immersed in boiling water – for a short period of time to destroy all the bacteria and enzymes which cause the produce to start to deteriorate as soon as it has been picked. If vegetables are not blanched, or you do not blanch them for long enough, the enzymes will continue to be active during storage. This can result in loss of colour and flavour and the vegetables becoming tough. The timing is crucial when blanching and will vary from vegetable to vegetable.

Asparagus	small stalk	2 minutes
	medium stalk	3 minutes
	large stalk	4 minutes
Aubergine		4 minutes
Broccoli	florets	3 minutes
Beetroot	small	25–30 minutes
	medium	45–50 minutes
Brussels sprouts	small	3 minutes
	medium	4 minutes
	large	5 minutes
Cabbage	shredded	1½ minutes
Carrots	tiny, whole	5 minutes
	diced or strips	2 minutes
Cauliflower	florets	3 minutes
Celery		3 minutes
Collards		3 minutes
Corn on the cob	whole	4 to 6 minutes
Globe artichoke		7 minutes
Green beans		3 minutes
Greens like spinach		2 minutes
Jerusalem artichoke		3–5 minutes
Kohlrabi	whole	3 minutes
Mushrooms	whole (steamed)	5 minutes
	button (steamed)	3½ minutes

Mushrooms	slices (steamed)	3 minutes
Onion	rings	10–15 seconds
Parsnips		2 minutes
Shelled peas		1½ minutes
Snow or sugar snap peas		2–3 minutes
Courgette	slices or chunks	3 minutes
Sweet peppers	strips or rings	2 minutes
Turnips		2 minutes

After vegetables are blanched, you need to cool them quickly to stop them from overcooking. Do this by plunging them in a bowl of ice-cold water for the same amount of time as the blanching. Make sure you drain and dry them thoroughly on paper towels and then put into suitable freezer bags or containers.

Storage life

It is very important to make sure you put a date on your freezer packs as food only has a certain storage time before it starts to deteriorate or go rancid. If you are unsure of the quality, check the colour and smell of the produce once it has defrosted. If you find there is a rancid odour or the product has discoloured, then it is probably safer to throw the item away.

If you have a power cut, a freezer full of food will usually keep for about two days if the door is kept shut. If the freezer is only half-full, then the food will last about a day. If the freezer is not full, quickly group packages together so they will retain the cold more effectively. Separate meat and poultry items from any other foods so that if they begin to thaw, their juices will not drip and contaminate the rest of the food in the freezer. Never refreeze food that has thawed.

I am going to end this section with a list of foods and the recommended storage time to maintain the highest quality and nutritional value. It might be a good idea to put this on your labels alongside the date, so you know exactly when to use it by.

Fruit and vegetables

Fresh fruit and vegetables will usually keep in the freezer for up to 12 months without deteriorating.

Cooked dishes

Casseroles and stews	2 months
Flans and pies	2 months
Ice cream, sorbets, and mousses	3 months
Cooked, sliced meat in gravy	2 months
Meat pies	2 months
Pancakes	2 months
Pasta dishes	1 month
Pâté	1 month
Pizza	1 month
Rice	1 month
Soup	2 months
Steamed or baked puddings	2 months

Dairy products

Butter or margarine	6 months
Hard cheese	3 months
Cream	6 months
Eggs (do not freeze in shell)	12 months
Milk	1 month

Fish and seafood

Crab, crayfish, and lobster	cooked	1 month
	raw	3 months
Mussels (not in shells)		2 months
Oily fish such as herring, mackerel, salmon		2 months

Oysters (not in shells)		1 month
Prawns and shrimps		1 month
Smoked fish		2 months
White fish		3 months

Meat, poultry, and game

Cubed meat		2–4 months
Ham and bacon	sliced	6 weeks
Mince		1 month
Sausages and sausagemeat		1 month
Steak and chops		6 months
Chicken, guineafowl, and turkey		6 months
Duck and goose		6 months
Grouse, partridge, pheasant		6 months
Rabbit		6 months
Venison		12 months

Baked items

Biscuits		2 months
Bread		1 month
Breadcrumbs		3 months
Croissants		1 month
Cakes (without icing)		4 months
Cheesecake		1 month
Choux pastry		1 month
Danish pastry		2 months
Fruit pies	cooked	4 months
	uncooked	2 months
Pastry cases		4 months
Sandwiches		1 month
Scones		2 months

Chapter Seven

Frugal with
your Finances

Frugal with your Finances

Money can buy you a house
But a home it cannot buy
Money can't buy happiness
Nor can it keep you spry
Only spend what's in the coffers
And beware of those 'special offers'.

You have all heard the saying 'Look after your pennies and the pounds will look after themselves', well there has never been a truer statement. Money can become a major source of stress as it is a huge part of your life. Unless you are lucky enough to have inherited a large fortune or won the national lottery, we all have to find ways of earning enough money to make our lives comfortable.

In granny's day, few women worked outside the home and they juggled their lives around housework, children, shopping and the general running of the household. They were totally reliant on their husbands for money and usually had to survive on a minimal amount of housekeeping. They were definitely frugal with their finances, a lesson that perhaps we could all learn from our ancestors. They planned their menus carefully and used up any leftovers; nothing was ever wasted. Clothes were mended and worn until they were threadbare and shoes were given new soles and heels rather than thrown out because their owners were bored with the style. Luxuries were rare, but if people were lucky enough to have some money left at the end of the month, these special treats were really appreciated.

I am starting this section with a brief look at an average weekly expenditure at the beginning of the 20th century. To those of you who are not old enough to remember old money, a brief explanation might help. Old money – pounds, shillings, and pence or LSD (libra, solidus, denarius) – was the currency until the UK went decimal (100 pence to 1 pound) on 15 February 1971. The coins in circulation before this date included a halfpenny piece, a penny, a threepence, a sixpence or tanner, one shilling, two shillings, and a half crown.

4 farthings = 1d or old pence
12d = 1/- or shilling
5/- = 1 crown
2/6d = half crown
20/- = 1 old pound
240d = 1 old pound
£1 1s = 1 guinea

Banknotes started at the ten shilling note (50p in today's money), which disappeared in 1971 and was replaced with a fifty pence coin. The £1 note was withdrawn by the Bank of England in 1988.

AVERAGE WEEKLY EXPENDITURE c.1900

ITEM	SHILLINGS	OLD PENCE
Meat	4	0
Bread (about ten loaves)	2	3½
Flour	2	0
Vegetables	1	4
Butter	1	0
Fruit	1	6
Milk	0	1½ per day
Tea (half a pound)	1	0
Cocoa (half a pound)	0	6
Sugar (four pounds)	0	10

ITEM	SHILLINGS	OLD PENCE
Soap (one and a half pounds)	0	6
Washing soda and starch	0	½
Candles	0	1
Paraffin (half a gallon a fortnight)	0	3
Coal (one cwt)	1	3
Beer (three pints at 3½d)	0	10½
Rent (weekly)	5	6
Boots and shoes (for entire family)	1	8
Clothes (men)	1	0
Clothes (women and children)	2	0
School fees	0	4

When I started work at the end of the 1960s I was earning a staggering £7 6s a week and I used to budget my housekeeping to £4 a week. The first one-bedroom flat I bought with my husband in Hertfordshire cost £4,000, which at the time seemed an enormous debt to have hanging round our necks. We ran one car, but only used it when we had to, and clothes were a luxury if we had money left at the end of the month – which was very rare. I always kept a notebook of exactly what I had spent and never owned a credit card. The rule my husband and I stuck to was that if we didn't have the money we didn't spend.

Today, loans are easy to come by, people tend to live by credit, and luxuries are taken for granted. I would like to ask – are people any happier? I don't think so. Life seems full of stress and people don't take the time to sit and relax anymore. Maybe we should all take a step backwards and think of ways we can improve our lives and ask ourselves whether we really need a wardrobe full of new clothes or a kitchen full of gadgets, many of which gather dust anyway. Perhaps a good place to start is to take control of our budget and make sure we live within our means.

Try these few simple steps to start with:

- Set up a realistic weekly budget and stick to it.
- Don't spend more money than you have in your accounts.
- Teach yourself to use credit cards sensibly.
- Pay your bills on time each month.
- Don't take out a lot of hire purchase agreements that you are going to struggle to pay.
- If your debt gets out of control, seek some financial help before things get any worse.
- Always use a shopping list when you go grocery shopping so that you don't end up buying lots of things you don't really need. Try to use a supermarket that you know, so that you are not tempted to walk up and down the aisles. This could only tempt you into deviating from your shopping list.

Balancing your spending

Although you can keep track of your accounts online these days, I would still recommend keeping a note of your monthly spending, balancing against money coming in. This way you will quickly realize whether you are living beyond your budget. Make a list of all your regular monthly outgoings and then you will know exactly what you have left to spend on essentials and non-essentials. Here are a few examples:

- Rent or mortgage
- Gas
- Electricity
- Telephone
- Insurance
- Licences (car and television)
- Loan payments
- Travel (essential travel to and from work)

Non-essential items could include:
• Holidays
• Shoes and clothes
• A new gadget

Remember, you also need to take into account any unplanned expenditure such as repairs to the house or car, emergency dental treatment, or having to replace something like a washing machine. Ideally, you should put something away each month to allow for such occasions.

How to budget
When you start planning your monthly budget, make sure it is realistic and that it is a figure that you will be able to stick to. Until you get back on your feet you might have to forego a few luxuries, so write a list of the things that are most important so that you know that your money is going towards the expenses that matter the most.

• Write down your monthly income but do not include any overtime or bonuses as these cannot always be guaranteed.
• Write down what you would like to achieve financially by the end of the year.
• Study your bank statements over the last year to see where your money is really going. Are you overspending on certain non-essential items?
• When working out your budget allow for items that are only paid quarterly, half-yearly, or annually.
• Make sure your budget can meet your essential needs. If not, you might need to think about how you can earn extra money or possibly change your job.

- Ideally, your expenses should be less or at least equal to your total income.
- Try to save as much money as you can every month; even a small amount can make a great difference in the long term. Why not set up a direct transfer into a savings account each month; that way you won't be so tempted to spend it.
- Try to limit spending on credit cards. If it is necessary to use one, then try to pay it off at the end of each month so that you do not accrue too much interest.
- Finally, make sure you review your budget regularly to see if it is really working for you.

A bank overdraft

A bank overdraft is a way of borrowing money and is an agreement between you and your bank. It allows you to be overdrawn by a figure agreed with the bank for a certain length of time. This can be a cheap way of borrowing if you only want to borrow small amounts of money and it is far better to negotiate a figure with your bank than allow your account to go regularly overdrawn which would incur higher interest charges. The bank will set the amount of money you can borrow which they call your 'overdraft limit'. Before you borrow the money find out what rate the interest will be charged at and for how long you can borrow the money. If the bank has given you a variable rate, they are obliged to inform you if they wish to vary the rate at any time. If the bank is concerned about your ability to repay the debt, they can either reduce your overdraft limit or demand that you repay the loan in full. Make sure you do not exceed the limit they set you and keep the bank happy by regularly topping up your bank account so they can see you are a responsible customer.

The danger of credit cards

Although credit cards – managed properly – can be very useful in helping you to manage your money by delaying certain payments, the danger of overspending and accumulating high interest debts is very real. Credit card companies carefully work out the minimum repayment figures that are designed to make your debt last for a long time, giving them a much higher profit margin. Let's say you borrow £1,000 at 20 per cent APR over the period of a year; you will actually be paying £200 in interest. Of course the longer you leave the debt to build up, the more interest you will pay as you will end up paying interest on the interest as well.

Quite simply, if you do want to use credit cards, the quicker you repay the less it will cost you. If you can manage to pay the full amount at the end of each month, then you will accrue no interest at all. If you can't do that then try to repay as much of the loan each month as you can afford, as the more you pay the faster the debt will disappear. Another solution to keeping on top of your credit card bills is to set up a direct debit so that you will never miss a payment or make a late payment.

Kids and mobile phones

The first encounter with debt that your children will experience will probably be with a mobile phone bill that has got out of control. Today, a mobile phone is an essential accessory to a child, regardless of age. I have seen children as young as seven, busy texting a friend, completely unaware of how much it is costing their parents. Until your child starts working you will be responsible for their mobile phone account so it is up to you to take control from the start. Make sure you set up an account that is prepaid and suggest that your child contributes a portion of their pocket money towards the bill. This will help to give them some understanding towards managing their money from a young age. Make sure you communicate with your child and develop a set of rules right from the outset.

Chapter Eight

Social Etiquette

Social Etiquette

'Excuse me miss, you've dropped your hanky'
Said the kindly man, so tall and lanky
'Why thank you sir,' the lady replied
As he handed it back all dewy eyed.

British people have a reputation for being polite – or at least the majority of them – and for their punctuality. Social etiquette is just knowing how to behave without making a fool of yourself and treating others as you would like to be treated. The concept of the 'British stiff upper lip' evolved during the Victorian era and is something that has never completely gone away. It simply meant that a person should keep their decorum under all circumstances and emotions were things you kept to yourself. Strangers were rarely spoken to unless you were introduced to them, or they happened to be standing next to you in a queue. Social etiquette and good manners are often forgotten in the bustle of modern life, so a quick reminder of how to greet strangers, how to eat in a posh restaurant, and how to treat your dinner guests won't go amiss. As children we were always taught to 'mind our Ps and Qs', which meant to always remember to say 'Please' and 'Thank You'. We would get a clip behind the ear if we dared to forget. Another thing my granny was adamant about was that we should never 'snatch' anything from someone's hand, no matter how desperate we were to get hold of it. She would take it away and put it out of reach if we dared to snatch. We also had to behave like little angels if anyone came to dinner and told that we 'shouldn't speak unless we were spoken to'. I think many of these old social etiquettes have now been brushed aside, but we can still teach our children good manners, without going over the top. Remember that we, as adults, are their role models. The basics of good manners are really common sense and if you practise them in your everyday life they will come naturally. How much nicer to be remembered for your nice manners that for being labelled 'rude'.

Timekeeping

It is considered to be the height of bad manners to turn up late for an appointment, so if you know you are going to be late – even by a few minutes – make sure you call the person you are meeting to let them know.

• Make sure you are prompt for any professional appointments, say with a doctor, dentist, or solicitor, as these people generally work to a very tight schedule. Not only could you throw out their appointment system for that day, you may also be charged for a missed or late appointment.

• If you are invited to a public function like a wedding, a funeral or a christening, or you are going to a concert, a film or an operatic performance, make sure you arrive a few minutes early.

• If you are invited to a dinner party, cocktail party, or an afternoon tea, make sure you arrive during the hours specified.

• If you are invited to someone's house for a party and it says '7.30 for 8.00', make sure you arrive no later than 7.50. If the invitation states the word 'sharp', make sure you arrive in plenty of time.

Queuing

Have you ever thought about how long you spend in queues? We have been described as a nation of queuers as we stand in line for just about anything – buses, supermarket checkouts, cinema or theatre tickets, the post office, to enter a sports stadium, etc, etc. Queuing is a bizarre activity when you think about it and if you want to upset an Englishman, just try and push your way in front of him while he is queuing. That is definitely a 'no-no'!

Correct forms of greeting
- A handshake is the most common form of greeting in the UK and is customary if you are being introduced to a stranger. Only shake their right hand with your right hand, never the left.
- A kiss is reserved for someone that you know well or a member of your family. A kiss on one cheek is usually sufficient.
- The usual formal greeting is 'How do you do?' followed by a firm handshake. Alternatively, greet them with 'Nice [or Pleased] to meet you' or use the appropriate time of day as in 'Good morning [afternoon] [evening]'.

Visiting someone's house
- If you have been invited to someone's house for a meal or party, it is good manners to take a gift for the host and hostess. Acceptable gifts are a bunch of flowers, a box of chocolates, or a bottle of wine.

- If the evening has been a great success and you would like to show your appreciation, then a thank-you card is always a nice gesture.

- Men should always take their hats off before entering someone's house.

Being polite
- If someone is blocking your way, it is polite to say 'Excuse me' rather than just push past them.

- Make sure you always remember to say 'Please' and 'Thank you' otherwise you could be labelled as rude.

- Remember to cover your mouth when you cough, sneeze or yawn.

- If you accidentally knock into someone, remember to say 'Sorry'.

- This is a custom that is sadly dying out, but it was always polite for a man to open a door for a woman and allow her to enter first.

- Spitting in the street is considered to be the height of bad manners.

- It is not polite to ask a lady her age!

- It is not polite to stare at anyone in public, especially if you are travelling on buses or trains. Always try to avert your eyes or have something to read.

- If you accidentally burp or pass wind in public, say excuse me politely and walk away to save yourself further embarrassment.

Eating etiquette
- If you have been invited to dinner, let your host know well in advance if you have any special dietary needs, such as being vegetarian.

- Always wait until your host is seated and wait until they start eating before taking your first mouthful.

- Make sure your mouth is empty before you take a sip of your drink.

- Always use a knife and fork unless you are at a party that is serving finger food.

- Always remember to say 'Thank you' whenever you are served something.

- When eating bread rolls, make sure you break off a small piece before putting on any butter. Eating it whole is considered to be bad manners. Take a small amount of butter and put it on the side of your plate as this allows the butter dish to be passed around without getting full of crumbs.

- When you have finished eating, place your knife and fork together with the tines of the fork facing upwards on your plate.

- Never lick or eat from your knife.

- Do not put your elbows on the table while you are eating.

- Never lean over someone else's plate to reach something; always ask politely if they would mind passing the item.

- Never talk with your mouth full.

- Never use your fingers to push food onto a spoon or fork.

- Do not blow your nose on your napkin, this is only for wiping your mouth or fingers.

Tipping

Many people seem to be uncertain about the amount of money they should leave as a tip. If you are in a restaurant, first check the bill to make sure they have not included a discretionary service charge or that it says 'service is included'. If gratuities are left to the customer's discretion, the normal amount to add is 10 per cent of the total bill. The same applies to taxi fares, just add 10 per cent. If you are in the hairdressers or, say, you want to tip a hotel porter, then usually a couple of pounds is adequate to say thank you. It is more polite not to show the person the money, simply slip it into their hand.

Chapter Nine

Entertaining Without the Stress

Entertaining Without the Stress

The table's laid, the food is cooking
The house is tidy, and the music addressed
Then you remember your hair's unkempt
And here's the arrival of your first guest!

Are you one of those people who loves to entertain but always gets in a fluster at the last minute? I have long envied those people who remain as calm as a cucumber and welcome their guests looking immaculate, with a house that looks like it has come out of a page from *Home and Garden*. I will never be one of those people, but I have always been congratulated on wonderful food and my friends and family say they would never miss an opportunity to dine at my house because they might miss out on all the fun and laughter. A compliment indeed, and one that I cherish. I have taught myself, over the years, not to tackle anything complicated unless I know I have plenty of time and, hey!, suppose they do turn up while I am still in my jeans and slippers, they have come to see me and not my wardrobe. I will often choose a menu that allows me to get things ready in advance, so don't go for some fancy soufflé that has to be eaten as soon as it comes out of the oven, you will be heading for disaster. I will give you a recommended menu and recipes at the end of this chapter, and it is one that I know you will be remembered for.

Channel your skills

When planning a dinner party, sit down and make a list of your positive skills, things that you know you are best at doing. If you are creative you might like to make some fancy place names for fun or do something really ornate with the napkins. If you are really creative then you might like to put a menu together as this makes quite a nice talking point at the start of a meal.

If your forté is puddings, then go overboard and make a really fancy pudding, or if you are better at main courses then use this to show off your cooking skills and leave the other two courses simple.

I don't have a fancy dinner service, but I do try and colour coordinate my tables so they look nice, and, if I have room, a small pot of fresh flowers in the centre of the table finishes it off nicely. I have always been known for being a little 'quirky' so if the dinner plates aren't all the same, or the cutlery doesn't quite match, it really doesn't matter and makes for a far more relaxed evening.

One evening that really went off with a bang was when I decided to hold a Murder Mystery dinner one New Year's Eve. The whole evening was planned so that everyone took a part and the courses were served between each 'act'. The invitations went out well in advance so that everyone had time to choose their costume, along with a brief outline of what was expected of them. There were ten people in total and the whole evening was a laugh from start to finish and the meal lasted over several hours.

Don't forget to be a host

In all your preparations, you have to remember to be the perfect host. Your guests will not want you to be permanently in the kitchen as this can quickly make them feel uncomfortable. After all, it was your idea to hold the dinner party in the first place, so they need to feel that you are enjoying the occasion. Even if you feel a little tense, don't show it; the aim of the perfect host is to feel relaxed and this can only come if you are prepared in advance. Do not try anything you haven't cooked several times before, otherwise this could lead to a lot of stress. Try any new recipes out on your hubby or family first and if they are a success and easy to prepare then put them on your list of 'safe' menus. It is quite normal for a guest to ask if they can do anything to help you, but if you find they are asking on more than one occasion this could indicate they think you are getting flustered. Assure them that everything is under control and that you can manage, although you can say that they can help when it comes to serving as this is a time when you can do with an extra pair of hands.

Remember your limitations

• Take into account the size of your kitchen and the amount of workspace you have.

• Allow for the size of your oven and the number of hotplates so that you don't find yourself with too many things to cook and not enough room to do it.

• When planning your menu, make sure you have sufficient cooking pans that are the right size.

• Limit the number of guests to the size of your dining table and the number of chairs you have available. Remember to take into account that you will need room for side plates, glasses and any extra dishes that you are going to serve up.

• Choose your menu carefully around the amount of time you have to spare. If you work full time you will probably be tired at the end of the week, so make sure you choose simple, easy to prepare courses.

• If you are really strapped for time, don't feel bad if you have to cheat a little. Either get one or more of the courses cooked by an outside caterer, or make something well in advance and put it in the freezer so that there is no preparation. No one ever needs to know your little secret!

• I think the golden rule to cooking is to clear up as you go along. Make sure everything is washed up and not piled up in the sink. Keep your worktops clear to give yourself plenty of room to work.

• Check and double check that you have all the ingredients as you don't want a disaster after the shops are shut.

Choosing the menu
• Try to balance your menu and, where possible, choose fresh, natural produce that is in season.

• Try to combine different colours, flavours, and textures that compliment each other and if you decide to serve a salad, never add the dressing until the last minute otherwise it will wilt and go soggy.

• Try to avoid a main course recipe that involves a lot of last minute preparation as this will put too much pressure on you when your guests arrive.

• Make sure you check that none of your guests has specific dietary requirements that will need to be included or excluded from the menu.

• Do not try to incorporate too many different flavours in any one dish, but allow the simple, fresh flavours to enhance the dish. Do not mix different cultures such as, say, a Chinese starter mixed with a French main course; try to stick to a certain theme.

- Don't think you have to go over the top to impress; good quality ingredients cooked well are sufficient and do not have to be expensive.

- Don't try to go all gourmet and over the top with a lot of fancy garnishes. These will do nothing to enhance the dish, so let the flavours speak for themselves.

Planning the drinks
Because I am teetotal and actually dislike the taste of wine – weird I know – I always leave this to my husband. He always asks what I am serving and then will choose the drinks accordingly and this of course is one less worry for me.

- The general rule of thumb is white wine for white meat or red wine for red meat, but of course there can be exceptions to the rule. Rosé wine is a great accompaniment to fish and white meat, and works well with most light flavoured foods such as chicken, pork, salads, rice dishes, cheese, and bread. The slight sweetness in rosé wines means that they do not complement spicy foods.

- Remember to have some grape juice or other non-alcoholic beverage to offer as some guests may be driving or, like their host, do not enjoy a tipple.

- Always make sure you have a jug of iced water on the table, as many people like to drink this to clear their palates or to dilute some of the alcohol.

- If you are intending to have a cheese course then you might like to have some port handy or a nice Sauterne to go with the stronger blue cheeses.

• The fact is, there are no hard and fast rules as to pairing food and wine and I would say that you should serve the combinations that work well for you. Keep your guests' tastes in mind, and if you know them well enough, you will know exactly what they will appreciate.

Napkin folding

If you really want to impress your dinner guests why not have a go at folding some napkins. This diamond fold is not only pretty it also serves as a cutlery holder. Just follow these simple steps:

1. Fold the napkin in quarters, so that the open corner faces away from you.

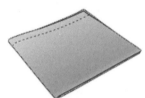

2. Fold down the top layer of fabric, so that the corner reaches almost all the way to the bottom.

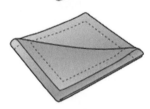

3. Fold down the next two layers in the same way, creating a cascade effect.

4. Flip the napkin over.

5. Fold the napkin into two thirds by folding back the right and left sides.

6. Flip the napkin over and slip the cutlery inside the pocket.

How to lay the table

- To make your table look really glamorous, treat yourself to a really crisp-looking tablecloth which should be large enough to hang over the edge by about 30 cm (approximately 1 ft). Make sure it is ironed to perfection well in advance and a felt cloth underneath will help to protect your table from any hot dishes.
- If you decide to use your tabletop, then you will need place mats to stop hot plates from damaging the wood.
- If you wish to place hot dishes on the table, then also buy a thick table runner, preferably of a bright colour, which is placed in the centre of the table. Metal trivets also come in handy for this.
- When placing the cutlery, always start from the outside of the plate and move towards the inside. The cutlery to be used first, for example a soup spoon, should be placed furthest from the dinner plate. The dessert spoon and fork should be placed at the top of the dinner plate in a horizontal position. Although this all might sound a bit pretentious, it actually helps your guests who otherwise

could be unsure of which cutlery to use for which course.

- If you are serving a starter of, say, melon or grapefruit, then it is a good idea to bring a small spoon to the table with the dish.
- Make sure the blades of all the knives face towards the plate, with the blunt surface facing outwards.
- Small side plates should be on the left with a butter knife placed diagonally across the plate.
- All glasses are kept on the top right-hand side of the dinner plate. Always provide a water glass and, depending on the type of wine you are serving, use a larger wine glass for red and a smaller one for white.
- Napkins can either be folded and placed on the side plate, or have a go at the one described earlier as you can use this on one side to put the cutlery in.
- Flower arrangements or any seasonal decorations should always be the centrepiece of the table.
- Unless you intend to put everything on the plate before you serve, any serving dishes such as those for vegetables, casseroles, gravy boats, etc should be placed in the centre of the table, ready to be passed around for the guests to help themselves.
- Make sure that all condiments are on the table before you start the meal.
- Wine should be left on the side somewhere. Red needs to be served at room temperature, but make sure the white is well chilled before your guests arrive.

Of course, all these formal settings go out of the window if you decide to hold an Oriental evening, when it will be chopsticks all round!

Making lists
I always find the easiest way to make sure my dinner parties go off without a hitch is to make lists of what I need to buy and what I need

to do and then stick to them religiously. Writing the approximate amount of time you think it will take beside each job gives you a rough idea of how much time you need to put by. Let's start with the shopping list, though. Go through each recipe and write down all the ingredients you need and then go through your cupboards to see which ones you have and which ones you will need to buy. I normally shop the day before I intend to start cooking, so that I give myself a free day to get everything ready.

My suggested menu

The following is only a suggestion, but is one that is really easy to do well in advance and leaves you feeling in control on the day of the party. There is no need to stick religiously to the recipes given here. You might like to put your own personal touches to them, but until you are confident with flavours and textures err on the cautious side.

If your guests are late

You will always get people who turn up early and those who turn up notoriously late. Early I can cope with as I am usually ready well in advance, but late I feel is inexcusable unless there is a genuine reason for their tardiness. Should you wait for them before sitting down to dinner, risking that the food could be spoilt or should you just go ahead anyway? This is my ruling, and one you may well wish to ignore, but I generally feel that 30 minutes is considered long enough to wait for guests to arrive before the meal is served. When the guests do eventually show up, I am always polite and say something like, 'I am glad you could make it, we are just about to embark on the second course!' Once they realize that you haven't actually been waiting for them and you were enjoying yourselves anyway, they might feel the need to be more punctual next time. Of course, you could just invite them an hour ahead of your planned schedule next time!

THE STARTER

Butternut Squash and Apple Soup

This soup is a wonderful combination of vegetables which can be made in advance and warmed up just before the guests arrive. The quantities given here are for four people and it is great served with some fresh crusty bread, warm from the oven. It is quite filling so I would suggest just small bowls for a starter, unless you have guests with very large appetites.

Ingredients
30 g (1 oz) butter
2 large leeks (white and pale green parts only), chopped
1 large onion, chopped
1 large potato, peeled and cubed
275 g (10 oz) butternut squash, cubed
2 carrots, diced
1 cooking apple, peeled, cored and sliced
1 litre best chicken stock
125 ml (4 fl oz) single cream
salt and pepper to taste
½ tsp hot smoked paprika
chopped chives, to serve

Preparation method
1. Melt the butter in a large saucepan and cook the onions and leeks until they turn translucent, about 5 minutes.
2. Add the potato, squash, carrots, apple, and chicken stock. Bring to the boil and then reduce heat until it is simmering. Cover and cook until the vegetables are soft, approximately 20 to 30 minutes.

3. Once the mixture has cooled a little, purée in batches in a blender, or directly in the saucepan using a stick blender. Season with salt and pepper and paprika to taste.

4. Half an hour before your guests arrive, put the soup on the stove to warm up. Just before serving add the cream and do not allow it to boil. Ladle into bowls and serve garnished with chopped chives.

THE MAIN COURSE

Beef Wellington

You might feel this is a little extravagant if you are catering for a lot of people, but if it is a small dinner party, it is easy to do and can be prepared in advance just like the soup. I tend to make it on the morning of the party and leave it in the fridge until the evening when I let it come to room temperature and put it in the oven while we are having starters. It is very easy to make and is my *piéce de resistance* and the dish my son-in-law always asks for whenever they are invited over to dinner. If I am on the phone to my daughter making arrangements, I can hear her husband yelling 'Wellie, Wellie' in the background – needless to say I always succumb under pressure. The quantities here will cater for six people.

Ingredients
1 kg (2 lb) best quality beef fillet
3 tbsp olive oil
250 g (9 oz) assorted mushrooms (e.g. chestnut, porcini, wild)
50 g (2 oz) butter
12 slices prosciutto
1 pack best quality smooth pâté
500 g (1 lb) packet of puff pastry
2 egg yolks, beaten with 1 tsp water

Preparation method

1. Preheat the oven to 220°C (200°C if fan assisted), 400°F or gas mark 7. Brush the beef with some olive oil and season with black pepper. Roast for 15 minutes for medium-rare or 20 minutes if you like it medium. When you have cooked the beef as you like it, remove it from the oven and chill in the fridge for 20 minutes.

2. While you are waiting for the beef to cool down, chop the mushrooms finely. Heat two tablespoons of olive oil and all the butter in a large frying pan and fry the mushrooms on a medium heat until cooked through. Remove from the pan, season, and allow the mushroom mixture to cool down.

3. Lay two pieces of clingfilm on a large chopping board, overlapping slightly. Lay the pieces of prosciutto on top of the clingfilm, overlapping slightly, in two rows. Spread the pâté over the top of the prosciutto until it is covered by a thin layer. Next spread half the mushroom mixture over the prosciutto and pâté. Place the cooled beef on top of this and then spread the remainder of the mushrooms on top.

4. Using the clingfilm as a guide, gently roll the prosciutto around the beef until it forms a nice sausage shape. Twist the ends of the clingfilm to tighten it and then chill the beef while you roll out the puff pastry.

5. Dust a large board with some flour and then roll out a third of the pastry into a rectangular strip approximately 30 x 18 cm (12 x 7 in). Place this on a non-stick baking tray.

6. Roll out the remainder of the pastry to a rectangle of approximately 36 x 28 cm (14 x 11 in).

7. Remove the clingfilm from around the beef fillet and then place the beef in the centre of the smaller piece of pastry. Brush all round the edges of the pastry and the top and sides of the wrapped fillet with the beaten egg yolk.

8. Using a rolling pin, carefully lift the larger piece of pastry and gently drape it over the fillet, pressing well into the sides. Trim the edges, but not too close to the meat, and then seal by pressing a fork all around the joins.

9. Glaze the 'Wellie' with the remainder of the egg yolk and then make diagonal scores in the top. If you want to be really creative, make some leaves out of a spare piece of pastry and place them on top for decoration.

10. Chill in the refrigerator for at least 1 hour, but can be left for up to 24 hours before cooking.

11. When you are ready to cook, preheat the oven to 200°C (180°C for fan assisted ovens), 400°F or gas mark 6. I like to let the meat come to room temperature and then brush with a little more egg yolk before baking. Cook until crisp and golden – 20 to 25 minutes for medium-rare or 30 minutes for medium. Make sure you allow it to stand for 10 minutes before serving in delicious thick slices.

I usually serve this with light, fluffy dauphinoise potatoes, baby carrots and some young asparagus shoots (if they are in season).

Dauphinoise Potatoes

This is by far the quickest and easiest method to make dauphinoise potatoes and, like most of my party dishes, can be made in advance to save a last minute rush. The potatoes stay really soft and moist as they absorb much of the liquid, but you will need to make sure you buy waxy potatoes so that they will retain their texture. This quantity will serve four people as a side dish. I don't really remember who gave me the idea of cooking the potatoes first, but it certainly cuts down on cooking time, gives me excellent results every time, and allows me to prepare the dish the day before.

Ingredients
600 g potatoes (Maris Piper work well)
350 ml milk
350 ml double cream
1 bouquet garni
90 g Gruyère cheese, grated
Salt and ground black pepper

Preparation method
1. Peel the potatoes and then slice into equal slices about 1 cm (0.3 in) thick. Rinse and pat dry on some paper towel.
2. Bring the milk and cream to the boil in a large saucepan, add the bouquet garni and seasoning. Simmer for a couple of minutes.
3. Gently place the potato slices in the milk mixture and simmer gently for about 7 minutes, or until the potato is just tender. You do not want to overcook them at this stage otherwise they will start to break up.
4. Drain the potatoes in a colander, making sure you catch all the milk in a bowl for later use.
5. Gradually start to layer the potatoes in a shallow, ovenproof dish. In between each layer, sprinkle a layer of the grated cheese and a little seasoning before pouring a little of the saved milk over each layer, too.
6. When you have used up all the potatoes, sprinkle the remainder of the cheese on top and then pour a little more of the milk around the sides, just enough to moisten. Chill in the refrigerator until you are ready to bake.
7. This dish will take 10 to 15 minutes to cook at 200°C, 400°F or gas mark 6. You will know when it is ready when the cheese starts to turn a wonderful golden brown. Allow it to stand for about 10 minutes before serving. I guarantee this one will be a big hit with all your guests.

THE DESSERT

Fruit Pavlova

This is an old family favourite and one my children always asked me to make for Sunday dinner. It is a slight variation on the regular pavlova and it has crunchy meringue outside and a fluffy centre which make a perfect combination. Choose fruit that is in season to decorate; raspberries and strawberries are my personal favourite, but anything sharp goes well with pavlova.

Ingredients
3 egg whites
250 g (9 oz) caster sugar
2 tablespoons water
3 teaspoons cornflour
½ teaspoon vanilla essence
1 teaspoon vinegar
⅛ teaspoon salt
Fresh fruit of choice

Preparation method
1. Preheat the oven to 140°C, 275°F or gas mark 1.
2. Grease a baking tray, line it with baking parchment and then sprinkle it with a little water.
3. Whisk the egg whites in either a large glass or metal mixing bowl until they are foamy in appearance. Gradually add the sugar and continue to whisk the eggs until stiff peaks form.
4. Whisk in water, then gently fold in the cornflour, vanilla, vinegar, and salt, making sure you are not too heavy handed as you don't want to lose the air you have already incorporated.
5. Pour the meringue mixture onto the middle of the baking tray.

There is no need to spread it out as this will happen as the pavlova starts to cook.

6. Cook in the preheated oven for 45 minutes, then turn the oven off and leave the pavlova in the oven until it has totally cooled down. Turn it upside down onto a plate and top with whipped cream and fruit of your choice.

TIP: Do not overbeat your egg whites as this can make them a little flat and grainy. Also, when you are whisking in the sugar, only add a little at a time and beat well between each addition. Finally, make sure you do not get any of the egg yolk into the whites, otherwise they will not get fluffy.

THE CHEESE COURSE

If you really want to impress your guests, leave a little extra time to make these extra special little biscuits to go with the cheese. They are delightfully crisp, light, and cheesy.

Cheesy, Herby Biscuits

Ingredients
100 g (4 oz) butter
100 g (4 oz) flour
100 g (4 oz) cheddar cheese, grated

Toppings
Fennel seeds, caraway seeds, poppy seeds, cumin seeds, and paprika

Preparation method
1. Put the butter, cheese, and flour into a food processor and whiz until the mixture forms a smooth dough.

2. Roll the dough into a long log with a diameter of around 5 cm (2 in). Wrap the log in clingfilm and put in the refrigerator for around 30 minutes.

3. When you are ready to cook the biscuits, preheat the oven to 190°C, 375°F or gas mark 5.

4. Line two baking trays with baking parchment.

5. Unwrap the log and cut it into thin slices as evenly as possible, and lay them on the baking trays.

6. Make an egg wash by mixing one egg yolk with a tablespoon of water. Brush the tops of the biscuits with the egg glaze and then top each one with a topping of different seeds and paprika so that you have a nice assortment.

7. Bake for around five minutes or until they are golden brown. Store the biscuits in an airtight tin until you want to use them.

Easy Crusty Bread

You will probably think I have gone mad if you are new to entertaining and say, 'She must be joking!' Trust me on this one, this is the best crusty bread you have probably ever tasted and you don't even have to knead it! All you need is time to allow it to do its work – 24 hours actually – but if you do feel you can cope with making your own bread then it will be a wonderful accompaniment to your soup. Home-baked bread tastes better than anything you can buy, and you can always tweak the recipe by adding, say, some olives or sun-dried tomato. This is another recipe sent to me by my sister in America, so once again it comes with US cup measurements.

Ingredients
3 cups white bread flour
¼ teaspoon instant yeast
1¼ teaspoons salt

Preparation method

1. In a large bowl combine the flour, yeast, and salt. Add 1⅝ cups of water and stir until it is well blended. The dough will appear very sticky at this stage. Cover the bowl with clingfilm and leave it to rest for at least 12 hours (18 hours is even better) at room temperature.

2. The dough is ready when the surface is dotted with little bubbles. Lightly flour a work surface and place the dough on it. Sprinkle it with a little more flour and then fold it over on itself once or twice. Cover the dough loosely with clingfilm and leave it to rest for about 15 minutes.

3. Using just enough flour to stop the dough from sticking to the surface, gently shape it into a ball. Cover a cotton tea towel with plenty of flour or bran, place the dough in the centre, and dust with a little more flour or bran. Cover with another tea towel and leave it to rise for another two hours. When it is ready, the dough will have more than doubled in size and will not readily spring back when poked with a finger.

4. Heat the oven to 230°C, 450°F or gas mark 8. Put a heavy covered pot, either cast iron, glass, or ceramic, in the oven as it is heating up. When the dough is ready, take the pot from the oven, and then lift the dough from the tea towel and gently put it into the pot. Don't worry if it looks a bit of a mess at this stage, cooking will even it out.

5. Cook with the lid on for 30 minutes, then remove the lid and cook for a further 15 to 30 minutes or until the loaf is browned.

There is nothing difficult about this recipe all you need is time to leave it to rise. This can be an advantage because it means you can prepare all the other recipes in the meantime. I hope you enjoy my suggested menu and I am sure your guests will be only too delighted to be invited back for a second time.

Well . . . you've made it to the end
And I hope the journey was fun
You've learned a few tips on the way
And so my job is done.
Make sure you try some of these hints
Because that will make me smile
Knowing I managed to help you
Has made my job worthwhile.

I hope you found a few useful hints in this book as I know I have had fun writing it and sharing pieces of information that have been stored in the old grey matter for eons. I never stop learning and, because the memory is not as sharp as it was, I write ideas down in my journal alongside photographs to remind me of special occasions. Every time my grandchildren draw me a picture it takes pride of place, as do the many thank you cards from friends and family with their heartfelt messages.

When you are young, life seems endless and infinite, but as you advance in years, time becomes very precious. I want to remember as much as I can about the things that have happened in my life and by writing it down it brings all the memories flooding back.

When my children were small I used to write stories for them and get them to illustrate these themselves. I feel happy and proud that those books – although a little tatty and thumbed – are still in use today and sit on the nursery bookshelves to be read at bedtime. Often my children say to me, 'Do you remember this?', or 'Do you remember that?' and I smile and say, 'How could I ever forget?'.

INDEX